5-00

ally Featherstone and Su Wall

PM 12/16

D0543969

WITH

Sounds
Fun

16–36
months

Published 2010 by A&C Black Publishers Limited
36 Soho Square, London, W1D 3QY
www.acblack.com

ISBN 978-1-4081-1467-4

Copyright © A&C Black Publishers Ltd 2010

Written by Sally Featherstone and Su Wall
Design by Trudi Webb
Photographs © Shutterstock, Fotolia and Rebecca Skerne

With thanks to the following schools for their help with the photos:
Valley Children's Centre (Rotherham) and Yarm Preparatory School (Stockton-on-Tees)

Printed in Great Britain by Latimer Trend & Company Limited

A CIP record for this publication is available from the British Library.

To see our full range of titles
Visit www.acblack.com/featherstone

Contents

Introduction

The best environment for communication

It is now well known that communication skills such as eye contact, body language, listening and speaking are at the heart of all learning and development. Children with good communication skills grow up to be confident members of society, who can use their skills to make the most of life inside and out of the education system. We also know that babies and children who, for various reasons, do not develop these skills in early childhood are at risk throughout the rest of their lives. They may fail to make strong relationships with others, they may be less successful in their working lives, and find learning much more difficult.

Such knowledge about language development has resulted in government initiatives such as *Every Child a Talker, Communication Matters* and *Letters and Sounds*, which are intended to support practitioners as they work with babies and children in the ever-increasing range of childcare provision. Some babies and children now spend more time in day - care than they do at home, so the role of practitioners in supporting language development is very important, not just for those children growing up in disadvantaged or lone parent families, but those where both parents work long hours, where the home language is not English, or where the many other pressures of modern life mean that families spend less time together.

While the environment for communication in the early years should ideally replicate the best home situation, there are some factors which practitioners in settings may need to take into account when evaluating their own settings. The impact of radio, television, computers, mobile phones and constant background music has had a significant effect on children's ability to listen, speak and concentrate.

- Practitioners should be aware of these features of home life and restrict the use of television and computers in their setting as much as possible. In fact, many experts say that babies and children should have little or no television or computer exposure until they are three years old. This ideal is perhaps unrealistic in children's home lives, but we should make every effort to counteract this in early years settings.
- Mobile phones, computer games and MP3 players are solitary occupations, often without the involvement of another person, and certainly without the added messages of eye contact, facial expression and body language. Practitioners should bare in mind that the parent who spends much of their time texting or listening to their iPod will not be communicating as much with their child.
- Background music from the radio or television disrupts attention and restricts hearing. Music is a useful tool for practitioners but it should not be used indiscriminately. Keep music at a suitable volume and for particular activities –don't use it as 'aural wallpaper'!

Dummies and pacifiers

Dummies and pacifiers can also be very damaging to language development, particularly when they are used all day. This use restricts the development of speech by reducing the muscular development within the mouth and tongue, as well as endangering the formation of teeth. Practitioners will need to handle this information sensitively when talking to parents, and encourage them to restrict the use of dummies and pacifiers to sleep time or when the child is distressed. Children who crawl, walk or run around with a dummy or feeding cup constantly in their mouth endanger their language development and may endanger their personal safety if they fall. Settings should consider whether to include guidance on dummies, pacifiers and feeding cups in their policies and procedures as well as in their prospectus or guidance to parents.

The role of the Key Person in communication

The role of key person is vital to the success of *Sounds Fun* activities. Close bonding between key adults and the babies and children in your setting will create a firm foundation for language development. Key members of staff know each child and their family well, and they are in a unique position to nurture language and social development. Their observations will be vital in deciding which activities to plan for the child, and they can create the warm, welcoming and informed link with the child's family.

The key child or key group is at the heart of these activities. They are ideal for key group times, so build them into your daily programme, using individual and small group times for talking, listening, singing and rhymes. Create comfortable places indoors and outside for these key times – settees, armchairs, swing seats, garden benches, bean bags, cushions and rugs are all useful places for language activities where babies and children feel at ease.

Remember that the language you use is crucial to babies' and children's own language development. Use appropriate language whenever you are with children, even if you think they can't hear or are not listening. Children are like sponges and they will soak up your language, whoever you are talking to, and whatever they appear to be doing at the time.

Some tips are:

- If you use 'baby language' such as 'baa-lamb', 'moo-cow' or 'quack-quack' you will restrict children's language development. As a professional you need to help children to learn and use the proper names for animals and objects.
- Don't use slang or 'street language', and discourage others in your setting from using it too. You may need to discuss this as a group and even decide which words are unsuitable. We sometimes use unsuitable words without thinking, and are surprised when children repeat them back to us, or use them in their play.
- Local words or dialect words are part of children's world, but you do need to help them to use a range of words, including alternatives to the local ones.

Introduction

Children with additional needs

As Key person you have a responsibility to identify, and if necessary seek help for, children with additional needs. Your setting will have a policy for the support of these children, and if you observe extreme difficulties you should follow the procedures in the policy.

However, some babies and children have developmental delays, which are less severe and can be supported by adapting the activities to make them simpler or less demanding. Other options include choosing activities from an earlier book, or limiting the length of time or the size of the group for the activities you choose. Observation, note-taking and consultation with colleagues and parents will help you to get the right match of activity for each child.

Taking the activities outside

Some children love being outside, are naturally more focused there, and learn best in an outdoor environment, where the sounds, sights, colours and smells are so different from indoors. Outdoor play is now a requirement within the Early Years Foundation Stage, and we have supported this requirement by embedding outdoor activities in all four Sounds Fun books. Each activity in each book has suggestions for taking the idea out of doors, regardless of whether you have a large or small outdoor area.

Some settings have ideal outdoor spaces but of course some of you are providing outdoor experiences in gardens, parks, playgrounds, community spaces or even the balcony of your flat! These are all suitable places for taking 'Talking Time' out of doors and we hope you will adapt the suggestions to fit your own circumstances.

Of course, every setting has its own policies and procedures for outdoor play, and we would strongly advise that you continue to follow these, as every setting is different. However, we would like to add some specific guidance for the 'Talking Time' activities, which we hope will help you to make the most of your outdoor area. Your outdoor area should include spaces for stillness and quiet reflection, away from the busy bikes and ball play. These places could include seats and benches, grassy areas, pop-up tents and other shelters, blankets, mats, cushions, sleeping bags, groundsheets or mattresses. Use these areas for individual or small group times for talking, listening, story telling or singing, and be there in all weathers and during all four seasons. A Place to Talk Outside by Elizabeth Jarman (Featherstone) has some excellent ideas for making sure outdoor spaces are the kind of places young children will develop their language skills.

Involving parents

These books contain a wealth of suggestions for working with parents, and simple ideas for activities parents will be able to do to support their children's learning. The section 'Involving parents' included with each activity suggests things that parents can do at home, things they can bring to show at the setting and other ideas for simple home-based resources.

How will 'Sounds Fun' activities help you?

This series of books is intended to help you help children with sounds, words, talking and reading.

The activities:

- expand the work you are already doing in your own setting to ensure that every child becomes a confident talker and listener – with the best foundations for later speaking, listening, reading and writing;
- support your work with individual children and groups within the Key person process;
- help you in your work with parents, who are children's first and most influential educators;
- provide stimulating and varied activities, carefully matched to the developmental stages in your setting, from babies to children of Reception age, where the activities will be useful support for your phonics sessions.

Which age range are the activities suitable for?

Every activity is presented in the same format to make it easier for you to use within your own planning framework. For ease of use, we have divided the activities into four age ranges, covering the whole of the Early Years Foundation Stage:

- Book 1 covers developmental stages 1 and 2: babies from birth to 20 months (Babies)
- Book 2 covers developmental stages 3 and 4: babies and children from 16 to 36 months (Toddlers)
- Book 3 focuses on development stage 5: children from 30-50 months (Pre-school)
- Book 4 focuses on development stage 6: children from 40 – 60+ months (Reception)

Of course, if you have children whose communication levels are high, you may want to dip into the next book in the series, and if you have children who have individual needs or would benefit from more reinforcement at an earlier stage, you can refer to earlier books.

What's inside each book?

Each book contains 35 activities, each on a double page spread and featuring:

- The focus activity (What you need, what you do and what you say);
- How you could **enhance** the activity by adding more or different resources;
- How you can **extend** the activity for older children or different sized groups;
- Taking the activity **outside** into your garden, a park or other play area;
- Suggestions for **songs, rhymes and stories**;
- **Key vocabulary and gestures** for you to use during the activity;
- Suggestions for **things to look for** as you observe the children during the activity (Look, listen and note);
- How to **use the activity with parents**, either by adapting for home use, or involving parents in your work in the setting.

Some activities will become favourites with the babies and children, and you will return to them again and again in your daily routine, building them into such times as snack, changing and rest times, as well as in the introduction to stories and song sessions.

Treasure baskets

This activity is suitable for one child or a small group of children.

What you need:

A small lined basket

A blanket

A range of natural objects including wooden spoons, ribbons, wooden pegs, natural sponge and brushes

A warm and safe area on the floor

Enhancing the activity

- Place a number of baskets next to each other so each child can have their own.
- Include shiny and metal objects.

♪ Sing a song about the object. Make it up if you can't remember one or use a nursery rhyme or your own words to a familiar tune:
Treasure basket, treasure basket,
Come and play, come and play,
You are so exciting, you are so exciting,
Play with me, play with me.

A treasure basket activity provides a lovely sensory session where children can explore a range of natural materials at their own pace, with the support of an adult.

What you do

1 Organise a range of natural objects attractively in the basket.
2 Put the basket on the blanket and sit the children next to the basket.
3 Sit beside the basket yourself.
4 Allow time for the children to start to explore the basket by themselves.
5 If needed, pick up an object and hand it to the children.
6 Only intervene if a child passes you an object or turns to you to involve you.
7 Watch the children closely and observe how they are investigating the basket.

Take it outside

- Always check to be sure children sitting on the ground are protected from the sun, from the damp and wind, from other children who may be playing nearby and from insects or other wildlife.
- Put the treasure basket on a waterproof picnic blanket in a shady, safe place on the grass under a tree or bush so they can also watch and listen to the leaves and the sounds.
- Make a treasure basket containing only natural objects from the garden.

Look, listen and note

Does the child...
- *Grasp and manipulate of objects of interest*
- *Interaction with other children, copying, taking turns, sharing?*
- *Stay engaged - for how long?*
- *Use a range of vocabulary used including describing words, object words, action words and prepositions?*

Key words and gestures

- Look
- Names of sounds
- Repeated sound and rhythmical phrases help children's language to develop.
- Use gesture and facial expression to reinforce what you say: 'Shall we explore the treasure basket?' 'What does that feel like?' 'Did you like the...?' 'It felt...' 'That's nice' 'soft, hard, shiny, dull, smooth, rough...' 'What's that?' 'It's used for...' 'Shall we share?' 'What do you think?' 'It's made from...'

Extending the challenge

- Develop a range of different baskets – objects from the kitchen and bathroom or seasonal objects.
- For older children:
  - Encourage the children to make their own treasure baskets.
  - Talk in detail about each item – what it is, what it is used for and where it comes from.
  - Visit the local shops and buy objects of interest to put in a treasure basket

Involving parents

You could...
- *Leave the activity on display and show the parents how to use a treasure basket.*
- *Talk to parents about using everyday materials and objects for this activity and display them attractively.*
- *Suggest they make their own treasure baskets at home with guidance from you.*

TOP TIP
Be aware of the safety of the objects within the treasure basket. Check regularly that they are still safe!

What's outside?

This core activity is suitable for one or two children.

What you need:

A large window

A blanket

This activity is a great way of extending the inside environment by bringing the outdoor environment in and is ideal for developing language through new words and experiences. You will need to choose a window that is from floor to ceiling or find a way of sitting so you can all see out.

Enhancing the activity

- Before you start the activity, go outside and move some natural items into view through the window e.g. a plant or a child's windmill.
- Get older children or adults to go outside and look into the window – play Peek-a-boo.

♪ Sing songs about what you have seen. If you can't remember one, make up a song or have a songbook to hand to look one up. You could try: *It's raining, it's pouring, I hear thunder, Five little leaves so bright and gay* (sung to the tune of *Five little ducks*) or *Two little dickie birds*.

What you do

1 Before you start this activity, look out of the window yourself. This is best if you get down to the children's level and see what they will be able to see.
2 Place a blanket in front of the window, preferably not in a draught.
3 Sit yourself with the children in front of the window, close to the glass to focus the children's attention on the view outside.
4 Talk about what they can see outside, such as 'Look, can you see the trees outside?'
5 Go on and describe what you can see: 'The trees are moving in the wind, can you see them? Look at the green leaves.'
6 Point and show where different objects are and ensure the children are able to focus on them nearby. (SF: sense?? On the ones nearby?)
7 Constantly observe the children. Praise and encourage them using your voice and reassurance with a cuddle.
8 With one child at a time, hold him/her closer to the window so they are able to touch and feel the window. Ask: 'Is the window cold?' 'What noise have you just made?'
9 Observe the children's responses and stop once interest has been lost.

Take it outside

- Extend the activity by going outside to look more closely at the things you could see from indoors.
- Let the children touch, feel and smell the objects they have seen, including trees and plants. Be aware and ensure the plants are soft and safe to be touched.
- Talk to the children: 'What does it feel like, is it soft, hard, cold...?' 'Can you hear the wind?'
- Make the most of spontaneous occurrences e.g. if an animal comes into the garden or if it's starting to snow or a rainbow appears in the sky.

Look, listen and note

Does the child...
* *Interact with other children copying, taking turns and sharing.*
* *React to different textures?*
* *Stay engaged - for how long?*
* *Use a range of vocabulary used – describing words, object words, action words and prepositions.*

Key words and gestures

* Use of the children's names
* Use gesture and facial expression to reinforce what you say: 'Let's have a look out of the window' 'What's that?' 'What can you see?' 'Can you see the...?' 'Well done, you are a clever girl' 'What does that look like?' 'What's the weather doing?' 'Is it raining?' 'Look at the rain drops'.
* Describe what you have seen: 'Look, did you see the dustbin lorry? It's emptying our bins.' 'Can you see and hear the children playing outside?'
* Maintain contact with the children and use different voice tones to keep their attention.

Involving parents

You could...
* *Talk to parents and demonstrate how to use the everyday environment with their child, bringing the outdoors inside.*
* *When at home, parents could put a child's chair next to the window so the child can sit and look outside whenever they like.*

Extending the challenge

* Bring items inside that you have spoken about (e.g. a selection of leaves) and place them on the blanket for the children to touch and feel, or bring snow into the water tray but be aware of how cold the snow is for very young children.
* For older children:
    * Look at the weather. Talk about the rain, sun, wind and snow. If it's raining, talk about the patterns on the windows and the noise the rain makes.
    * Go to the window at particular times of the day e.g. when the dustbin lorries are outside or the post person is delivering letters.

TOP TIP
Get down to the child's level to see what they can actually see out of the window before you start this activity.

Reflections

This core activity is suitable for one child from 16 months.

Mirrors are a very versatile resource and can be used with children in a variety of ways. In this activity, mirrors are used along with a variety of textures and shiny objects to look at and to explore textures.

What you do

1 Place the blanket in a safe, warm place.
2 Put the shiny items in a basket. A see-through container will allow the child to see all the items.
3 Sit on the blanket with the child and put the container next to you. Make sure you are comfortable and there is enough room to enjoy this activity.
4 Hold the mirror in front of the child's face talking as you do so: 'Look at you, can you see yourself in the mirror?'
5 If the child reaches out for the mirror, move it into contact with their fingers and hands and let them hold it, praising them for effort and talking about the mirror.
6 Use plenty of facial expression, using your eyes, eyebrows and mouth to express yourself through sounds and words as you look at each other in the mirror.
7 Shake the container to engage the child in something new, and bring one item of interest up for them to see.
8 Talk about what the item is – its texture and colour.
9 Allow time for the child to respond and explore.
10 Move the mirror up and down and look at the reflections. Ask: 'Can you see the reflection in the mirror from the...?'
11 Move on to the next item of interest and allow time for repetition.
12 Observe the child's responses and when it's time to finish, give the child a cuddle and lots of praise.

Involving parents

You could...
- *Leave the activity out and show the parents how to do it.*
- *Talk to parents about using everyday materials and objects for this activity.*
- *Display some suitable everyday objects to handle, and hang them low down where they will shine in natural light.*
- *Talk about the use of mirrors within the home, the bathroom, on dressing tables and in the car.*

Extending the challenge

- Let the children investigate the container themselves.
- Bring in torches, prisms and coloured paddles to reflect differently in the mirror.
- For older children
  - Cover a container or tough spot with foil and place the mirror and items of interest on the foil.
  - Turn lights off and shut curtains as you use torches, prisms, coloured paddles etc with the mirror and objects – watch for different reflections.

Look, listen and note

Does the child…
- *Grasp and manipulate objects of interest?*
- *Use a range of language: describing words, object words, action words and prepositions?*
- *Interact with other children, copying, taking turns and sharing?*
- *Stay engaged – for how long?*
- *Smile with enjoyment?*

TOP TIP

Ensure the mirrors you use are children's mirrors and are safe to use with babies.

Key words and gestures

- Use of the child's name
- Toy and object names
- Names of sounds
- Use gesture and facial expression to reinforce what you say: 'What colour is that, it's…' 'Can you hear the…?' 'How soft… hard … furry… rough is that?' 'Is it shiny… dull…?' 'Look at that lovely smile' 'I can hear you' 'Look at the colours reflecting' 'What colours can you see?' 'Look at the patterns' 'They are…' 'I can see you' 'Well done' 'Who's a clever boy/girl!' 'Look at the mirror' 'What can you see?' 'What happens if…?' 'Light, dark, reflecting…'

Take it outside

- Always check that children are protected from the sun, from the damp and wind, from other children who may be playing nearby, and from insects or other wildlife.
- Put the blanket on a waterproof picnic blanket in a shady, safe place on the grass under a tree or bush, and put an unbreakable mirror on the blanket so the child can see the trees and sky. Be careful that the sun doesn't reflect in the mirror.
- Hang shiny items of interest from low branches, including mobiles and old CDs.

Enhancing the activity

- Use a larger mirror or two mirrors, so you can include more than one child. Let the children explore items of interest together.
- Tie some bells on to ribbons to introduce new sounds as well as reflections and colours. Ensure the bells are secure.
- Look out for different textures of materials including crinkly paper, furry material and bought feathers – you will find new items of interest everywhere!

♪ Sing a song! Sing any baby nursery rhymes or your own words to a familiar tune. If unsure, keep a nursery rhyme book next to you.

Ready, steady, go!

This core activity is suitable for one or a small group of children from 16 months

What you need:

A strong cardboard box

A teddy bear

A doll

A hat

A warm, safe area on the floor

Enhancing the activity

- Help the children to take turns to sit in the box with teddy and dolly and join in the ride.
- Move the box about and round the room singing 'The wheels on the bus go round and round...'

♩ Using songs and rhyme

♩ Sing a song about the object. Make it up if you can't remember one or use a nursery rhyme or your own words to a familiar tune

♩ such as 'Miss Polly had a Dolly' or

♩ 'Teddy Bear, Teddy Bear'

Cardboard boxes are such a versatile resource which don't cost anything and can be used in such exciting ways. In this activity, the box becomes a bus and encourages the child to look, point and to use sounds and words as they play 'The wheels on the bus'.

What you do

1. Place the cardboard box on the floor and sit the teddy in the box.
2. Start to sing 'Teddy on the bus goes brrm, brrm, brrm... all day long' to the tune of 'The wheels on the bus'.
3. Offer more teddies or dolls to the children and encourage them to put them on the bus. Use short phases and natural gesture.
4. Sing 'Dolly on the bus goes bounce, bounce, bounce... all day long'.
5. As you do so, bounce the box up and down and encourage the child to bounce with you.
6. Give the child the hat and say: 'Let's put the hat on teddy'.
7. Sing 'Teddy on the bus wears a hat, wears a hat, wears a hat... all day long'.
8. Give the child the bag and say: 'Let's put the bag with the dolly'.
9. Sing 'Dolly on the bus is carrying a bag, carrying a bag, carrying a bag... all day long'.
10. Use pointing and natural gesture to help the child's emerging understanding of single object words and names.
11. Watch the children closely and observe how they are responding to the activity.

Key words and gestures

- Names of sounds
- Repeated sound and rhythmical phrases help children's language to develop.
- Use gesture and facial expression to reinforce what you say: 'Are you ready?' 'Lets sing together' 'Teddy, doll, hat, bag' 'What do you think?' 'What shall we have next?' 'Before, behind, empty, full, box' 'Let's' 'Look'

TOP TIP

Allow time for the child to respond and express themselves through their first words and gestures.

Look, listen and note

Does the child…
- *Grasp and manipulate objects of interest?*
- *Use their first words?*
- *Understand and follow simple instructions?*
- *Interact with other children, copying, taking turns and sharing?*
- *Stay engaged – for how long?*
- *Smile and laugh with enjoyment.*

Take it outside

- On a dry day, this is a lovely activity to take outside.
- Always check that children sitting on the ground are protected from the sun, from the damp and wind, from other children who may be playing nearby, and from insects or other wildlife.
- Put the cardboard box on a waterproof picnic blanket in a shady, safe place on the grass under a tree or bush and use natural objects from the garden to enhance the song.

Involving parents

You could…
- *Have the activity out and show the parents how to transform a cardboard box in to an exciting activity.*

Extending the challenge

- Introduce more objects for teddy and dolly such as shoes, a book, a cup etc.
- Use two or more boxes to include more than one child. The box becomes a train – 'The wheels on the train go…'
- For older children:
  - Ask the child to go and find objects themselves.
  - Use more challenging instructions.
  - Take teddy and dolly on an actual bus ride.
  - Paint and decorate the box before singing the song.

Look, over there!

This core activity is suitable for one child.

What you need:

Soft toys such as a teddy, rabbit or monkey

Toy telephone

A cup

A hat

A flannel

A warm, safe area on the floor

Enhancing the activity

- Hide cars, buses and lorries around the room. Play 'Look, I think it's over there', pointing to one of the vehicles.

- ♪ Sing a song about the object. Make it up if you can't remember one or use a nursery rhyme or your own words to a familiar tune such as Teddy Bear, Teddy Bear.

Using natural gesture and pointing will help children's understanding of their first words and is an integral part of the way you communicate with young children.

What you do

1 Hide the soft toys, peeking out from behind furniture around the room.
2 Give the child the hat and ask: 'Whose hat is this?' 'Is it for Teddy?' 'Where is Teddy?'
3 Encourage them to point towards teddy or another soft toy and to fetch the toy to have the hat put on.
4 Praise them for their efforts and don't forget to smile.
5 Point to the teddy saying 'Look, Teddy is wearing the hat'.
6 Continue to play the game, pointing to and choosing a soft toy to interact with by giving it a drink, washing its face or speaking to it on the telephone. Let the children fetch each toy as you talk about it.
7 Watch each child closely and observe how they are responding to the activity.

Take it outside

- On a dry day, this is a great activity to take outside. Hide the soft toys in the garden.
- Always check that children sitting on the ground are protected from the sun, from the damp and wind, from other children who may be playing nearby, and from insects or other wildlife.
- Use natural objects from the garden to enhance the activity.

Look, listen and note

Does the child…
- *Grasp and manipulate objects of interest?*
- *Use some first words?*
- *Understand and follow simple instructions?*
- *Interact with other children, copying, taking turns and sharing?*
- *Stay engaged – for how long?*
- *Smile and laugh with enjoyment?*

TOP TIP
Allow time for the child to respond and express themselves through their first words and gestures.

Extending the challenge

- Put everyday objects in a water tray to point to, name and show how to use.
- For older children:
  - Play with teddy and find body parts together e.g. 'Where's teddy's nose?' 'Where's your nose?'
  - Have a small group of children playing, sharing and taking turns.

Key words and gestures

- Look
- Names of sounds
- Repeated sound and rhythmical phrases help children's language development.
- Use gesture and facial expression to reinforce what you say: 'Are you ready?' 'Where is…?' 'Is he over there?' 'Can you see…?' 'Are they hiding?' 'What do you think?' 'What shall we have next?' 'Behind, next to, underneath, in front of' 'Let's'.

Involving parents

You could…
- *Talk to parents about the importance of pointing and natural gestures.*
- *Take and display photographs for parents to see.*

Light it up

This core activity is suitable for one or two children.

What you need:

A selection of coloured children's lights – ensure they are cold to touch

A blanket

A warm quiet area with minimum disruptions

Enhancing the activity

- Turn the main lights off, close the curtains and just have a selection of coloured lights on for the children to focus on.

- ♪ Sing a song about the lights. Make it up if you can't remember one or use a nursery rhyme or your own words to a familiar tune:
*Twinkle, twinkle little light, in the middle of the night,
Shining there for use to see
Shining, shining all for me,
Twinkle, twinkle little light, in the middle of the night.*

Children will react to lights from an early age. Sensory lights are very soothing and relaxing for children to gaze at, looking at reflections and colours. You can use a variety of brought sensory lights and objects, however everyday low wattage coloured lights can work just as well (SF – not sure what this means?). This is an excellent activity for children with additional needs.

What you do

1. Talk to the children as you gently sit them on the blanket.
2. Choose a coloured rope light and bring it near the children so they can see it.
3. Say: 'Look, it's a ...' Remember to smile and watch for their reactions.
4. Talk as you move the lights gently and switch them on and off.
5. Allow time for the children to look at the lights.
6. Introduce a bubble tube or another form of lighting and place next to them to look at.
7. Encourage the children to touch and feel the lights. Move the lights into contact with their fingers and hands, praising them for effort and talking about the textures and colours of the different lights.
8. Remember to use plenty of praise and facial expression while you talk about the lights.
9. When the children have lost interest, offer a cuddle and remember they will be relaxed and may benefit from some quiet time afterwards.

Extending the challenge

- Use a torch to shine patterns for the children to follow.
- Make the most of festivals – Christmas and Hanukah lights and Chinese lanterns.
- For older children:
  - Provide torches to explore the environment with.
  - During winter months at teatime, wrap the children up and take them outside in the dark to explore with lights and torches.

Look, listen and note

Does the child…
* *Track (follows movements with their gaze)?*
* *Use a range of language such as describing words, object words, action words and prepositions?*
* *Concentrate for long?*
* *Smile and laugh with enjoyment?*

Key words and gestures

* Use of the children's name
* Names of sounds
* Use gesture and facial expression to reinforce what you say: 'Can you see the lights?' 'What colours can you see?' 'Look, I can see red, blue…' 'The lights are beautiful' 'Let's turn the lights on' 'They are bright, dull, shiny…' 'What a clever girl/boy you are!' 'What happens if…' 'Can you touch that?' 'Is it dark, light?'
* Maintain contact with the children and use different voice tones to keep their attention.

Involving parents

You could…
* *Display a variety of lighting for parents to see including rope lights, fibre optic lights, tinsel and torches.*
* *Demonstrate to parents how to do this activity at home.*

Take it outside

* Depending on the weather, this activity may not work outside during bright days, but you could make a dark shelter with fabrics and use this outdoor lights.
* Always check to be sure children are protected from the sun, from the damp and wind, from other children who may be playing nearby, and from insects or other wildlife.
* Put the blanket on a waterproof sheet in a shady, safe place on the grass under a tree or bush so they can watch and listen to the leaves and the sounds.
* Hang rope lights from low branches or from a washing line or clothes airer. Make sure these are securely fastened and won't blow over. Stay close all the time.

TOP TIP
Check the lights are not too bright and are not shining directly in the children's eyes

We can paint with water

This core activity is suitable for a small group of children.

What you need:

Clean paint pots (one for each child)

Paint brushes (one for each child)

Children's waterproof aprons

A large jug or bucket

Water

Enhancing the activity

- Add bubbles to the water.
- Use bowls of water with a selection of sponges.

♪ Sing a song about what you are doing. Make it up if you can't remember one or use a nursery rhyme or your own words to a familiar tune such as *This is the way we paint...* to the tune of *Here we go round the mulberry bush*.

All children love to play and experiment with water. This activity provides children with the opportunity to paint using water and paintbrushes whilst playing outside. A lovely activity, no preparation needed, no cost, and no tidying away!

What you do

1 Before you start, check your health and safety policy on water play.
2 Take the group of children outside and talk about the fun of painting with water.
3 Help each child to put on an apron and give them a paint pot and paintbrush each.
4 Using the jug, pour a small amount of water in to each paint pot.
5 Allow plenty of time for the children to go and paint the garden using the water and paintbrushes.
6 Have extra water available to refill the paint pots and encourage the children to ask for more water.
7 Observe the children and talk with them but don't direct their imagination and creativity.

Key words and gestures

- Look
- Use of the children's name
- Names of sounds
- Use gesture and facial expression to reinforce what you say
- Maintain contact with the children and use different voice tones to keep their attention.

Extending the challenge

- Offer different size paint brushes – thick and thin
- Provide chalks for children to use for mark making
- For older children
  - Let them fill their own paint pots with water from a plastic jug.
  - Use chalk to make patterns on the floor and encourage the children to paint following the patterns.
  - Discussion about wet and dry and other changes.

Look, listen and note

Does the child…
- *Grasp and manipulate objects of interest?*
- *Understand and follow simple instructions?*
- *Interact with other children, copying, taking turns and sharing?*
- *Stay engaged— for how long?*
- *Use a range of language?*

Take it inside

- Have paint pots and brushes in the water tray. Make sure water tray is on a non-slip floor.
- Be careful that any spills of water are cleared away immediately to prevent children from slipping over.
- Variety of painting activities.

Involving parents

You could…
- *Display photographs showing parents the enjoyment of this activity and how easy it is to do at home.*
- *Suggest they could use paintbrushes at bath time!*

TOP TIP
Be aware of the safety of water play – never leave children alone with water.

Let's be creative

This activity is suitable for a small group of children from 16 months.

What you need:

A roll of paper (old wallpaper rolls are ideal)

A wide selection of markers – crayons, felt pens and coloured pencils

Sticky tape

Small baskets for the markers

A large, dry, flat area outside

Enhancing the activity

- Add even more different sizes and types of markers.
- Use different textures of paper – such as paper with bumps and patterns on the surface or rolls of pastel-coloured display paper.

♪ Make up simple songs as you work together, using familiar tunes to help. Try: '*See me draw a wiggly line, wiggly line, wiggly line... See me draw a wiggly line, can you draw one too?'*

Once this activity is prepared, very little interaction from you is needed. This activity will provide the opportunity for the children to choose for themselves what they want to do as they work alongside other children, negotiating and taking turns. There is no right or wrong way of doing this activity so it's perfect for all ages and needs of children. All you have to do is stay with them, watch and encourage.

What you do

1 Cover a large area outside with the paper and tape it down securely.
2 Sort and place the markers in baskets around the edge of the paper.
3 Talk to the children about the different types of markers available and show them the marks they make.
4 Stand back and allow the children plenty of time to make their own marks and patterns.
5 Observe and listen to the children as they make their marks and move about the paper, sharing and working with each other.
6 Talk to them about what they are doing, the marks and patterns they are making: 'That's a wiggly blue line'.
7 Encourage the children to put the lids back on the markers and return them to the basket when they have finished. You may need to help them.
8 Allow plenty of time for this activity, as more children will certainly want to join in.

Extending the challenge

- Have a basket of vehicles or bricks available, so they children can make roads and other scenes.
- Add some paint in flat containers, so the children can run the vehicles in the paint and then make tyre tracks on the paper.
- For older children
  - Introduce scissors, glue sticks and magazines, wrapping paper or greeting cards, so the children can extend their creativity by adding collage items.
  - Allow time for collaborative working, helping them to negotiate with other children as they share space and materials. Model the language of collaboration, by working alongside them.

Look, listen and note

Does the child...
* *Grasp and manipulate of objects of interest?*
* *Understand and follow simple instructions?*
* *Interact with the other children, copying, taking turns and sharing?*
* *Stay engaged? For how long?*
* *Smile and laugh with enjoyment?*
* *Use a range of language – describing words, object words, action words and prepositions?*

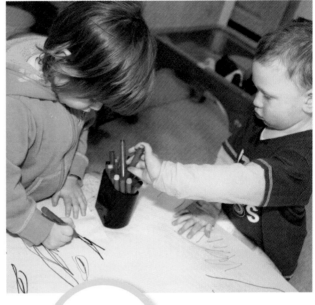

Take it inside

* Cover a large table with the paper and remove all the chairs so the children can move easily and freely around the table to cover it with their own marks and patterns.
* Put the activity on a vinyl, non-slip floor if you are using paints and glue.

TOP TIP
Remember, don't interrupt or direct this activity!

Key words and gestures

* Use of the children's name
* Use gesture and facial expression to reinforce what you say: 'Which one do you want?' 'What colour marker do you want to use?' 'Thick or thin?' 'Patterns, zigzag, wiggly, lines, circles, spots...' 'Put the lid back on the pen...' 'Well done' 'Tell me about the picture...'
* Language of negotiating: 'Please', 'Thank you', 'Can you pass me...?'

Involving parents

You could...
* *Display photographs showing parents the enjoyment of this simple creative activity and how children are beginning to work alongside each other, sharing and taking turns.*
* *Demonstrate to parents the range of markers available and the importance for children of having a range of mark making tools available so they can make choices, negotiate and work together.*

Teatime!

This activity is suitable for a small group of children from 18 months.

What you need:

Bread

Selection of appropriate spreads

Enough blunt knives (such as butter knives) for all the children

Table cloth

Paper plates

Enhancing the activity

- Make toast instead of sandwiches.
- Decorate the plates before making the sandwiches.
- Wash up in a big bowl all together, or let each child have their own bowl and wash their own equipment.

♪ Sing a song about cooking. Make it up if you can't remember one or use a nursery rhyme or your own words to a familiar tune, such as Pat-a-cake or This is the way we bake a cake... to the tune of Here we go round the mulberry bush.

Children love to cook and bake. Never mind the mess, both you and the children will have lots of fun as you make simple snacks for their tea!

What you do

1. Before you start, follow your health and safety policy guidance for using tools and preparing food. Check for any allergies.
2. Cover a large table with a clean tablecloth and tuck in the edges securely.
3. Show the children how to butter a piece of bread, talking through the process as you demonstrate.
4. Give each child half a slice of bread, a blunt knife and a small amount of butter.
5. Allow time for the children to spread the butter at their own pace. Some will get very involved and will take a great deal of time and care – don't rush them!
6. Discuss the different types of spreads for the sandwiches, let the children smell and taste them.
7. Encourage the children to choose and ask for the spread they want on their sandwich.
8. Offer help if needed with spreading the filling for the sandwich.
9. When the sandwiches are made, pass a plate to each child for their own sandwiches so they are ready for tea. The children will probably want to eat their sandwiches immediately, so be ready for this, and try not to make them wait!
10. Carry on making sandwiches until you have enough for tea or the children have lost interest.

Take it outside

- On a dry warm day, making tea outside is a lovely activity, but be aware of insects being attracted to food, and don't leave food out for long periods.
- Have a picnic on a rug outside for snack time or tea.
- Make or buy a bird table and make 'bird cake' for them to eat.

TOP TIP
Remember to take note of children's allergies.

Look, listen and note

Does the child…
* *Grasp and manipulate of objects of interest, tools and other equipment?*
* *Understand and follow simple instructions?*
* *Interact with the other children, copying, taking turns and sharing?*
* *Stay engaged? For how long?*
* *Use a range of language?*

Key words and gestures

* Names of movements (spread, scoop, cut, hold) and equipment (knife, spoon, plate, bowl)
* Use gesture and facial expression to reinforce what you say: 'Let's make some sandwiches for tea' 'What do you want in your sandwiches?' 'Which filling would you like?' 'Did you like that?' 'What does that smell/taste like?' 'Please and thank you' 'Bread, butter, jam, cheese…' 'Can you…?' 'Well done' 'You need to share with…'
* Maintain contact with the children throughout this activity. Use different voice tones to keep their attention and recognise their efforts and successes.

Extending the challenge

* Make vegetable soup. Encourage children to cut and chop a full range of vegetables: carrots, onions, potatoes, leeks, parsnips and tomatoes etc.
* Have a 'Teddy bears' picnic' with tiny sandwiches and cakes.
* For older children:
  * Bake cakes and biscuits. Discuss weighing and measuring. Talk about how the mixtures look before and after they are cooked.
  * Go shopping and buy ingredients for tea or for a picnic.
  * Follow a simple pictorial recipe.

Involving parents

You could…
* *Display photographs showing parents how enjoyable making tea with children can be.*
* *Encourage parents to let children help, even though it might take longer and the results may be a bit untidy!*
* *Compile a recipe book of simple recipes for parents to cook with their young children at home.*

Walks with talks

This activity is suitable for two young children.

What you need:

Two children

Yourself!

Enhancing the activity

- Go and meet your local shopkeepers.
- Bring back items of interest you have found. Autumn is a great season to collect items such as conkers, twigs and leaves, but each season will offer treasures to collect or photograph.
- Plan your walks at different times of the day/week – When is the post delivered? What time does the bus come? When is dustbin day?
- Visit your local library and share a story.

♩ Sing songs about what you have seen such as *It's raining, it's pouring, The wheels on the bus* or *Two little dickie birds*.

The local community is a valuable resource. Going for a walk with a couple of young children is a great way of communicating as you get some fresh air and model a healthy lifestyle. You don't need to go far. Little and often is the secret to these 'walks with talks'!

What you do

1. Before you start this activity check out your setting's relevant policies including those for general 'Health and safety' and 'Outings'.
2. Talk to the children about what you are going to do: 'Are you ready for a walk?' 'Where shall we go today?' 'Shall we go...?'
3. As you start to walk, talk about what you can see: 'Can you see the...'
4. Go on and describe what can be seen in more detail using descriptive vocabulary and pausing as you talk together.
5. Allow time for the children to talk to you about what they can see. Remember that young children may find it difficult to walk and talk at the same time!
6. Talk and show them different objects on your walk and stop to look more closely at objects of interest e.g. a garden gate, a spider's web, a post box. Look closely at a tree. Talk about the leaves, the bark, the fruits and any birds nesting in it.
7. Encourage the children to touch items of interest, listen to sounds and talk about what you can smell: 'Let's touch the bark of the tree' 'What does it feel like?' 'Can you hear the leaves moving in the wind?' 'Can you smell the flowers?'
8. On your walk, sing songs linked to what you have seen such as 'The wheels on the bus' when you pass a bus. Remember that doing two things at once can be difficult for children, so stop while you sing.
9. Go and visit local shops, such as the greengrocers or the Post Office.
10. Talk about each individual shop with the children – what they sell, where it comes from and who buys it.
11. Encourage the children to talk to each other as they walk and remember to talk to the children about anything and everything you see and do.

Take it inside

- You can have successful walks inside your setting, exploring different rooms, going round the inside or outside of the building, exploring offices and other areas that the children don't usually have chance to visit.

Look, listen and note

Does the child…
- *Understand and follow simple instructions?*
- *Interact with the other children, copying, taking turns and helping each other?*
- *Use a range of descriptive language when describing what they see on the walk?*
- *Enjoy walks and visits? Do they seem used to being out and about?*

TOP TIP
Make sure all the children know the local area within walking distance of your setting and their homes.

Extending the challenge

- Catch a bus with the children.
- Invite local professionals to your setting such as shopkeepers, the police or a librarian.
- Go out in all weathers – you can have very different experiences depending on the weather. Talk about the sort of clothing and footwear you need in different types weather.
- For older children:
  - Make a shopping list and go and buy from local shops. You could buy the ingredients to make a cake and then bake one.
  - Allow children to take photographs and display for all to see.
  - Walk to the park and have a 'Teddy bears' picnic'.
  - Practise simple road safety rhymes and codes.

Key words and gestures

- Use gesture and facial expression to reinforce what you say: 'What's that?' 'What can you see?' 'Can you see the…?' 'Can you hear the…?' 'What does that feel like?' 'What does that look like?' 'What's the weather doing?' 'It's a lovely sunny day' 'What a lovely smile' 'Are you talking to me?'
- Describe what you have seen in detail.
- Maintain contact with the child and use different voice tones to keep their attention.

Involving parents

You could…
- *Display photographs taken on the walk and show these to the parents.*
- *Encourage parents to take frequent short walks with their children. Many families only go out for shopping or specific visits and some have lost the art of going for a walk!*
- *When travelling in the car, encourage parents to talk about what they can see out of the window.*
- *Display maps and information about local facilities such as library services, recreation grounds, parks and nature reserves.*

Up and down

This activity is suitable for one small child from 16 months.

What you need:

One child

Yourself

Enhancing the activity

- Sit the child in your lap and play the game with a soft toy, lifting it up and down as you 'sing'.
- Use the song as part of daily greeting as the child arrives.
- Include 'Up and down' at changing time, or when you are moving from one activity to another.

♪ Sing a song. Make it up if you can't remember one or use a nursery rhyme or your own words to a familiar tune. You could sing: Up the tall white candle stick, Hickory dickory dock or Incy wincy spider.

Children gain a sense of security and safety from having plenty of one to one time with familiar adults. Children will love this activity as it gives them the opportunity to have direct contact with their key person through making sounds, naming, questioning and talking. These little games can be shared at all sorts of informal times – they don't have to be planned but they make a real difference to relationships.

What you do

1. Hold the child so you are face to face. You could hold them in your arms or under the arms
2. Look into their eyes and say: 'Hello name, hello name. Shall we play the up and down game?'
3. Lift the child up and down gently and say: 'Here we go up, up, up. Here we go down, down, down'.
4. Smile as you talk.
5. Lift the child gently round and round and say: 'Here we go round, round and round'.
6. Do this a couple of times. Use a simple tune or a sing-song voice as you talk.
7. Look at the child all the time as you play.
8. Imitate any sounds and words they make and encourage them to look at you as you 'sing'.
9. Give a loving cuddle after the game.

Key words and gestures

- Look
- Use of the child's name
- Repeated sound and rhythmical phrases help children's language to develop, so repeat the key words.
- Use gesture and facial expression to reinforce what you say: *'Can you see me?' 'Let's play the game' 'Are you ready?' 'One, two, three' 'Let's go' 'Up, down' 'Quick, slow' 'What a clever girl/boy you are!' 'What a lovely smile' 'Did you enjoy that? I did'*
- Keep your face where they can see you – you need to be quite near!

Look, listen and note

Does the child...
- *Use sounds, noises, gestures or words – which ones?*
- *Respond to sounds, songs, voices and movements?*
- *Copy and follow instructions?*
- *Respond by body movements, showing enjoyment as you play together?*

TOP TIP
Watch the child's responses and remember some children will like to be lifted softly and slowly – don't be over-enthusiastic!

Take it outside

- This is a perfect activity to play outside where you have the freedom to move about round the garden. You can add swooping and dipping movements when you have plenty of space.
- Always check to be sure children are protected from the weather, and be aware of other children who may be moving quite fast in the garden.

Involving parents

You could...
- Write the song and tune down for parents to take home, so they can make the 'up and down' song part of the way they lift their child from their cot/bed each morning.
- Listen to and copy the sounds and words their child is making.

Extending the challenge
- Play the game standing up so the feeling of 'up and down' is even greater.
- Count as you go up – be a rocket!
- Use different voice tones: loud, quiet and a whisper.
- For older children
    - Play the game more vigorously, but remember that very violent movements easily scare some children.
    - Let the child copy you and play the game with a toy or doll.
    - Have toys on strings or elastic to bounce gently up and down.

The fun of dens!

This activity is suitable for one child or a small group of children from 16 months.

What you need:

Big enough space outside to build a den

A large blanket

Household items such as pegs, rope, tape and clips

Enhancing the activity

● Drape a large blanket over a table, some big chairs or a clothes airer for an immediate indoor den.

● Use big boxes on their sides, and hang a thin drape over the open end. Join boxes together to make tunnels.

♪ Sing a song. Make it up if you can't remember one or use a nursery rhyme or your own words to a familiar tune such as *Peter hammers with one hammer, This is the way we...* or *My little house.*

Children love dens! They provide a secret area where children can explore and have lots of fun. Dens are easily made from many household items such as blankets, parachutes, fabric, rope, pegs and poles.

What you do

1 Before you start this activity, look around the environment to see where would be a good place to build the den.
2 Take the children outside and talk to them about making a den. Use your voice to engage the children and to share the excitement ahead of them.
3 Show the children the things you have collected and talk to them about what they are and how they can be used to make a den.
4 Carefully tie the rope securely between two bushes, trees, fences or other firm supports. Make sure there are no loose ends hanging down.
5 Hang the blanket over the rope and use pegs or stones to hold it down at the corners to make a tent shape.
6 Encourage the children to explore the den in their own time and at their own pace
7 Take a step back so you can observe the children from a distance without interrupting their play.

Extending the challenge

● Put a range of exciting items such as torches, magnifying glasses or a rope light in the den.
● Talk about the items you have used. 'What they are called?' 'What they are used for?' and 'What materials they are made from?'
● For older children:
   • Children will soon learn how to make their own dens if you provide plenty of open-ended materials and encouragement to construct them.
   • Use dens and shelters for games of ww'hide and seek'.
   • Have a tea party or picnic in your den, or offer some children's sleeping bags for a camping experience.
   • Have a box of dressing up clothes or a basket of books in the den.

TOP TIP
Remember not all children will feel comfortable in a small, enclosed den.

Look, listen and note

Does the child...
- *Use a range of language – describing words, object words, action words and prepositions?*
- *Interact with the other children, copying, taking turns, sharing and playing in role?*
- *Stay engaged? For how long?*
- *Work together, following instructions and making decisions?*

Key words and gestures

- Use of the child's name
- Toy and object names
- Names of sounds
- Repeated sound and rhythmical phrases help children's language to develop.
- Use gesture and facial expression to reinforce what you say: 'What's that?' 'Let's go and build a den' 'Come on, let's go' 'Where shall we build our den?' 'Let's have a look' 'What's that?' 'Can you make one?' 'What can you see?' 'Can you see the...?' 'Well done, you are a clever boy/girl.' 'Blanket, rope, pegs, stones...' 'What happens if...?' 'Where have you gone?' 'I can find you' 'I can see you'.

Involving parents

You could...
- *Take some photographs and display them so parents can see how you do the activity.*
- *Show the parents how to make dens from everyday household items – make dens in a bed under a duvet, under a table or in the garden.*

Take it inside

- Dens are easily transferred to inside but remember there must be enough room to move freely about and to make a den. You may need to clear away furniture and toys to ensure the children don't trip and fall over any obstacles. Try using pop-up tents indoors for a different experience.
- Be aware of the noise levels in an indoor den – are you in danger of disturbing anyone?

What can you hear?

This activity is suitable for one child.

What you need:

Your environment

Yourself

This activity is a great way for children to explore the surrounding environment through their hearing. Very little preparation is needed, no equipment is necessary and it can be done anywhere and at any time!

Enhancing the activity

- Listen out for noises from outside, for example traffic and birds singing.
- Get another adult to be in another room to make different noises – clapping hands, whistling, saying the child's name or playing a musical instrument.

♪ Sing a song about the object. Make it up if you can't remember one or use a nursery rhyme or your own words to a familiar tune such as Hickory, dickory, dock or I hear thunder.

What you do

1. Before you start this activity, look around the environment to see what makes noises and what you can show the child. Think about a variety of noises, which the child will be able to hear.
2. Walk around the environment with the child listening out for different sounds.
3. When you hear a noise, talk to the child: 'What's that?' 'Can you hear the...?'
4. Use your voice tone and facial expression to engage the child with the excitement of the new sound.
5. Go and find the object and reveal where the noise came from.
6. Talk about the object in more detail while the child is touching it, using describing words about textures, colours and what the object is used for.
7. Observe the child's responses and once the child has lost interest listen out for another noise as you move around the environment to the next object. Be aware that different objects will interest the child differently so allow plenty of time and watch their responses.
8. Use a variety of different objects to provide a variety of sounds and experiences including running water, the kettle, the radio, a mobile phone, the front door bell, other children playing, different toys and banging of doors.

Take it outside

- A lovely activity to do outside sitting under a tree in the shade.
- Talk to the child: 'Can you hear the wind?' 'Listen to the birds singing – what a beautiful song'.
- See also the activity 'What's outside the window?' on page 10.

Look, listen and note

Does the child…
- *Respond to noises by turning their head?*
- *Jabber loudly and freely using vocal tunes and phonetic units?*
- *Use recognisable words/two words together?*
- *Understand and follow simple instructions, such as, Let's go and find the noise.'*
- *Show a longer concentration span?*

Involving parents

You could…
- *Take some photographs and display them so parents can see how you do the activity.*
- *Demonstrate the activity and show the parents how to do it at home – it's a very easy and enjoyable one.*

Key words and gestures

- Use of the child's name
- Object names
- Names of sounds
- Repeated sound and rhythmical phrases help children's language to develop
- Use gesture and facial expression to reinforce what you say: 'What's that?' 'Let's go and find the noise' 'Come on, let's go' 'What does it sound like?' 'Is it loud, quiet…?' 'Let's have a look' 'What's that?' 'Can you make that noise?' 'What can you see?' 'Can you see the…?' 'Can you hear the noises from the kitchen?' 'Is it the dinner cooking?' 'Look how small it is' 'What was that bang?' 'What a lovely sound it is'.

Extending the challenge

- Make a sound box with some sound makers to choose from.
- Listen out for different weather sounds – wind, rain and thunder.
- For older children:
  - Make their own noises using their bodies – shouting, jumping, kicking, clapping and slapping.
  - Play 'Hide and seek' or a variation of 'Hunt the thimble' where you hide a small teddy or other object and use 'getting warmer', 'getting colder' to guide the child to the object.

TOP TIP
This activity can be done at anytime during the day, both inside and outside and it doesn't cost anything!

Let's grow our own

This core activity is suitable for two or three young children.

What you need:

A selection of seeds/plants (tomato plants and runner beans are good for starters)

A suitable area to grow (vegetable plot or tubs)

Gardening canes and wire, plant ties or string

A selection of tools (trowels, forks, spades and watering cans)

A wheelbarrow or large container

Suitable outdoor clothing (Wellington boots, children's gardening gloves)

Growing vegetables with children is a very rewarding activity for all of you. Children will love being outside and you can grow vegetables in pots or hanging baskets. Children will enjoy digging, planting and watering the plants.

What you do

1   Before you start this activity, follow your 'Health and Safety' policy on suitable plants to grow with children.
2   Prepare the vegetable plot or tubs before you start, by digging or filling with compost.
3   Show each item of equipment and the plants or seeds to the children. Make sure the children know the name of each tool. Explain what they are and what each one is used for.
4   Place all the equipment and plants or seeds in the wheelbarrow.
5   Put on your boots and coats and go outside together.
6   Encourage the children to dig the soil with trowels or small spades and forks, showing them how to do it if necessary.
7   Talk about the soil, textures, wildlife and the equipment you are using.
8   Plant the plants and gently secure them to the canes. Runner beans grow best up a wigwam of canes. Tomato plants need one straight cane to grow up.
9   Every day check on the plants with the children. Look for growth, remove weeds, water and feed them as they grow.
10 Once grown, pick the vegetables and allow the children to cook and taste their home grown food!
11 Remember to wash hands thoroughly after gardening, and to wash the vegetables well before cooking and eating them.

Key words and gestures

• Use gesture and facial expression to reinforce what you say: 'Are you ready?' 'Let's go and plant our plants' 'Soil, water, trowels, forks, watering cans, weeds...' 'Let's dig the soil over' 'There is a weed, let's pull that up' 'We need to look after the plants' 'Do you like...?' 'It's warm today, we need to water the plants' 'What does that feel like?' 'Is it hard, soft, smooth or rough?' 'Can you see they are growing?' 'Tall, small' 'Look what we have grown' 'Shall we go and cook them?'

Look, listen and note

Does the child...
- *Use a range of vocabulary?*
- *Concentrate for long?*
- *Show enjoyment with smiles and laughter?*
- *Understand and follow simple instructions in learning the names and purposes of the tools?*
- *Work together with the children, sharing, taking turns and copying?*

Enhancing the activity

- Grow cress inside – this is very quick and easy to grow.
- Include the vegetables in a cooking activity such as vegetable soup or a simple tomato sauce for pasta.
- Take photographs at each stage and display these or make a book.

Share songs and rhymes such as *This is the way we water the plants, One potato, two potato, Dingle, dangle scarecrow* or *There's a worm*.

Extending the challenge

- Grow more vegetables and fruit, thinking about seasons – strawberries for the summer and potatoes for the winter.
- Grow flowers – plant summer tubs with bedding plants and put winter bulbs in bowls inside.
- For older children:
  - Grow plants from seeds. Each child grows a sunflower and watches to see which sunflower grows the tallest.
  - Collect pips from fruits such as oranges, apples and avocados.
  - Talk and sing about the life cycles of plants.

Take it inside

- This activity can easily be transferred to inside.
- Plant small tubs or window boxes inside.
- Grow cress, beans, daffodils or hyacinth bulbs.
- Provide some houseplants to care for.

Involving parents

You could...
- *Ask parents to help with large vegetable plots.*
- *Reinforce how easy it is to grow fruit and vegetables at home.*
- *Do a gardening sheet for parents to take home. It could include: easy plants to grow, how to grow and look after them and songs related to this.*

TOP TIP
Remember not all children will have a garden so allow plenty of time for exploring and experiment.

I recognise that!

This core activity is suitable for one child.

What you need:

Recording equipment, such as a simple tape recorder, mobile phone or Dictaphone

Comfortable chair for you

A warm, safe quiet area

Enhancing the activity

- Bring in familiar objects from home that link with the sounds parents have recorded.

♪ Sing a song. Make it up if you can't remember one or use a nursery rhyme or your own words to a familiar tune. You could sing *Hush a bye baby* or *Miss Polly had a dolly*.

All children should grow up feeling safe and secure in a friendly and loving environment with familiar sounds and surroundings around them. This activity introduces sounds from a child's home in an environment where they are being cared for outside the home.

What you do

1 Allow the parent/carer to borrow your recording equipment to take home and record familiar sounds. This could include family voices, favourite lullabies and sound from pets or favourite toys.
2 In a quiet warm area, sit with the child in your lap with them facing you.
3 Say 'hello' to the child using their name and gently stroke their cheeks to engage their attention.
4 Softly play the child's familiar sounds from home 'Listen, can you hear...?'
5 Allow time for the child to listen and respond.
6 Use plenty of eye contact and smiles and offer a reassuring cuddle as you talk about the sounds you both can hear.
7 Join in with any familiar lullabies.
8 Maintain contact with the child and observe their reactions. Stop when the child has lost interest.
9 Give the child a hug.

Take it outside

- Encourage parents/carers to record familiar sounds from outside the home as well as inside.
- Choose an area outside with minimum distractions and listen to the recorded sounds.
- Always check to be sure children are protected from the sun, from the damp and the wind.

Look, listen and note

Does the child…

- *Recognise and respond to sounds, songs and voices?*
- *Concentrate for long? How long did it take them to respond?*
- *Show enjoyment with smiles and laughter?*
- *Use recognisable words/two words together?*
- *Understands simple comments and questions such as 'Did you hear…?'*

TOP TIP
Ensure there are minimum distractions and the child can clearly hear the sounds.

Extending the challenge

- Record familiar sounds from your setting and encourage parents to use them at home.
- For older children:
  - Make their own sound recordings using a children's tape recorder.
  - Share and explore different sounds with other children.

Key words and gestures

- Use of the child's name
- Toy and object names
- Names of sounds
- Repeated sound and rhythmical phrases help children's language to develop.
- Use gesture and facial expression to reinforce what you say: 'What's that?' 'What can you hear?' 'It's a…' 'I can hear your… can you?' 'Well done, what a clever boy/girl' 'What a lovely smile you have' 'Listen' 'Hush' 'Can you hear me?' 'It sounds like…' 'That was lovely'
- Make sure they can see your face.

Involving parents

You could…

- *Encourage parents to share experiences with you to allow you to understand home life.*
- *Ask them to bring in items of interest such as food and costumes from different backgrounds/ cultures.*

Funny bunny

This core activity is suitable for one young child.

What you need:

A collection of small soft toys

A quiet place on the carpet or soft chair/settee

Enhancing the activity

- Play 'Peek-a-boo' games with the child as you talk and name the toy.

♪ Sing any songs and rhymes with the children e.g. *There's a worm, A sailor went to sea, sea, sea* or *She sells seashells*.

Making up rhyming words and using this to create funny names for things helps young children to fine tune their listening and join in the fun!

What you do

1 Sit comfortably with the child and look at the toys together, picking them up and feeling them.
2 Now choose one toy and introduce it to the child: 'Hello name, I'm Funny bunny or Ready teddy or Soggy doggy'.
3 As you introduce the toy, make it 'walk' across the carpet or sofa towards the children.
4 Keep saying the silly rhyme as the toy advances.
5 When the toy gets to the child, make the toy tickle their tummy.
6 Repeat the game with another toy.
7 Praise verbal and non-verbal responses.
8 Repeat until the child begins to lose interest.

Key words and gestures

- Use of the child's name
- Use gesture and facial expression to reinforce what you say: 'Are you ready?' 'Let's have some fun' 'Let's do some silly rhymes' 'Can you say that?' 'Well done' 'Can you copy me?' 'What a good boy/girl you are' 'Listen' 'Peep-po' 'Does it rhyme?'
- Maintain contact with the child to keep their attention.

Take it outside

- This activity can easily be transferred to outside.
- Always check to be sure children are protected from the sun, from the damp and wind, from other children who may be playing nearby, and from insects and other wildlife.

Look, listen and note

Does the child…
* *Respond to sounds, songs and voices?*
* *Show enjoyment with smiles and laughter at the funny sounds and names?*
* *Use recognisable words/two words together?*
* *Understands and follows simple instructions, such as 'Can you hold Ready Teddy?'*

Extending the challenge

* Play together with a pop-up toy or a Jack-in-the Box, sharing the anticipation.
* Introduce silly noises as well as silly sounds.
* For older children:
  * Children can make up their own names for toys and objects
  * Some children will love the sounds of silly rhymes and songs and will sing and say them when they play by themselves

TOP TIP
This is a perfect time for lots of fun and laughter!

Involving parents

* *Parents could watch their child having fun doing this activity.*
* *Encourage them to play silly word and sound games with their children at home.*

Let's make some noise!

This core activity is suitable for one or a small group of children.

What you need:

A small blanket or piece of soft material

A warm, safe place

A number of small, cleaned empty water bottles, dried carefully

A selection of small dried materials such as dried pasta, small stones, lentils and sand

Glue

Enhancing the activity

- Add coloured water to the dried materials in the bottles.
- Use shiny objects, beads, or glitter.

♪ Sing a song or rhyme such as: *I am the music man, I can play on the big bass drum, If you're happy and you know it...* or *This old man, Ten green bottles.*

TOP TIP
Make sure the tops are securely glued on!

Children love to hear, play and enjoy the different sounds of music. You don't need to have expensive shop-bought musical instruments. Why not make some of your own for the children to enjoy!

What you do

1 You need to make sure that the bottles make different sounds by using different quantities of materials and mixing the materials together. Put some of the materials in each bottle. Put a different material in each bottle, then shake it and see what sound it makes.
2 Once you are happy with the sounds, glue the top securely on each bottle and leave to dry.
3 Sit the children on the blanket and talk to them about the musical instruments you have made.
4 Introduce one bottle at a time by shaking it gently near the children.
5 Use plenty of facial expression and eye contact so the children are engaged and concentrating. Watch their responses.
6 Let them feel the bottles, praising them for effort and talking about the sounds you are making.
7 Introduce another bottle sound and repeat. Let each child have a turn with their own bottle.

Take it outside

- This is a lovely activity for outside, where children can make as much noise as they like, and take the bottles with them as they play.
- Always check the bottles are safe, with lids securely fixed.

Look, listen and note

Does the child...
- *Respond to sounds, songs and voices?*
- *Show co-ordination of movement as they shake the bottles?*
- *Concentrate? For how long? How long until they respond?*
- *Show enjoyment with smiles and laughter?*
- *Understand and follow simple instructions e.g. 'Can you shake the bottle?'*

Key words and gestures

- Use of the child's name
- Object names
- Names of sounds
- Repeated sound and rhythmical phrases, such as 'shake, shake, shake the bottle' help children's language to develop.
- Use gesture and facial expression to reinforce what you say: 'What's that?' 'Can you copy me?' 'Let's do this together' 'What sounds does that make?' 'Is it noisy or quiet...?' 'Can you hear the sound?'

Extending the challenge

- Make up a simple song or rhyme such as *Shake the bottle, shake the bottle, shake, shake, shake.*
- Let the children explore the bottles by themselves.
- Play some music with a strong beat as you play the shakers together.
- For older children:
    - Make two bottles the same. Can the children recognise the same sounds?
    - Make the bottles together!

Involving parents

You could...
- *If you take some photographs and display them, parents can see how you do the activity and appreciate how much fun simple sound makers and musical instruments can be.*
- *Demonstrate the activity and show the parents how to improvise at home – perhaps using saucepans and spoons.*
- *Make a booklet of rhymes and songs for parents to use at home as they sing along to home made musical instruments.*

Puddles!

This core activity is suitable for a small group of young children.

On a wet day, there is only one activity worth doing and that's to go outside and splash in the puddles! This activity is all about enjoyment as well as singing, talking and rhyming!

What you do

1 On a rainy day, help the children to put on their Wellington boots and waterproofs.
2 Make sure they are well protected and won't get cold in the rain.
3 As you take the children outside, talk to them about what you are about to do 'Are we ready, let's go and find some puddles!' Use your voice tone to gain their interest and excitement.
4 Walk, dance and skip together looking for puddles.
5 Splash as you find the puddles. Make sure you join in too!
6 Allow plenty of time for the children to enjoy the puddles.
7 Talk to the children about what they are doing – splashing, kicking and jumping in the puddles.
8 Look at and talk about the patterns and reflections in the puddles.
9 If it's raining, dance and sing with the umbrellas 'I'm singing in the rain'.
10 Take photographs of the puddle fun.
11 When you come inside, make sure the children are dry and warm – perhaps have a hot drink while talking about the puddles.

Key words and gestures

- Use of the child's name
- Use gesture and facial expression to reinforce what you say: 'Are you ready?' 'Let's have some fun' 'Let's do some splashing' 'Can you do that?' 'Well done' 'Can you copy me?' 'What a good boy you are' 'Listen' 'Look' 'Can you see the patterns? They....' 'Look at the reflections' 'Can you see the colours?' 'Are we getting wet?' 'Let's dance, jump, kick...' 'What happens if...?'
- Stay with the children to keep their attention.

TOP TIP

A perfect time for lots of fun but remember never leave a child alone near water!

Look, listen and note

Does the child…
* *Enjoy this simple traditional activity?*
* *Understand and follow simple instructions?*
* *Share, take turns and copy other children?*
* *Use new language?*

Take it inside

* This activity can be transferred to inside with some careful planning. Follow your Health and Safety policy on safety of water, then set up a small paddling pool inside on a non-slip floor and enjoy the water experience with no shoes or socks on. Remember to wipe up any spills immediately.

Extending the challenge

* Drop sticks or pebbles into the puddles and see what happens.
* Watch the rain from inside. Look at the raindrops on the window and the patterns they make.
* Look at the photographs you have taken and talk about what it was like to splash in the puddles.
* For older children:
  * Look at and talk about all types of weather.
  * Ask where the puddles have gone.
  * Experiment with water – what happens if…

Involving parents

You could…
* *Display the photos you have taken and show parents the fun of a wet rainy day and jumping in puddles.*
* *Encourage parents to take their children out in the rain and have some fun too.*

What does that feel like?

This core activity is suitable for one or a small group of young children.

What you need:

A range of materials to explore, such as wet and dry sand, warm water, furry material, straw and shredded paper

A large container for each texture, such as builder's trays, washing up bowls or deep trays

Baby wipes or a bowl of soapy water and a towel

Camera

A warm environment

Enough space to ensure safety

Take it outside

- This is a great activity to take outside.
- Let the child explore and feel various materials outside including wet and dry grass and mud. Follow your health and safety policy when exploring plants and other natural materials.

This activity will help develop children's sensory awareness by providing a range of textures for them to explore using their feet and toes.

What you do

1 Place the materials in the containers. Ensure the containers are large enough to allow the child to stand in them and move around.
2 Take off shoes and socks and roll up trousers.
3 Hold the child under their arms, carefully move them over the containers and place their feet in to the first one. Make sure the child is facing you.
4 As they explore each container, talk to the child about what it is and what it feels like: 'Look, here is some dry sand, can you feel how soft it is on your toes?'
5 Watch their response! Take photographs.
6 Talk about the texture in more detail while the child is standing in it, using describing words about what it feels like, the colours and materials. Use plenty of voice tone and facial expression to keep them engaged.
7 Praise them for their responses, words, expressions or movements.
8 Move on to the next container and be aware that different materials will interest the child differently.
9 Observe the responses of each child and once interest is lost, carefully remove them from the container, saying 'Did you enjoy that?'
10 Give a reassuring cuddle as you clean and dry their feet.

Extending the challenge

- Experiment by adding a second substance e.g. water in the sand, beads in shaving foam.
- Make footprints and patterns in the substances.
- For older children:
    - Put some materials in see-through containers and let them choose what they want to try.
    - Use the seasons to introduce different materials e.g. autumn fruits or snow in winter.
    - Develop a mud garden or a sensory garden.
    - Cover a large area outside in backing paper and do footprints with paint or water.

Look, listen and note

Does the child…
- *Respond to sounds, songs, voices and experiences*
- *Concentrate — for how long does he/she they continue to explore the materials?*
- *Enjoy the activity?*
- *Use recognisable words or put two words together?*

Enhancing the activity

- Use larger containers such as a 'tough spot' to allow more than one child to join in at any one time. Extra adult supervision may be required to help, especially with cleaning feet afterwards.
- Explore the materials using hands and fingers.
- Use the outdoor environment to introduce new materials and textures (see 'Take it outside').

♪ Sing songs about what you have seen. Have a songbook to hand to look one up or sing *Oh I do like to be by the seaside.*

Involving parents

You could…
- *Display some photographs to show parents what fun this activity is.*
- *Talk to the parents and demonstrate how this activity can be adapted for doing at home, indoors or in the garden.*

TOP TIP

There may be some children who don't enjoy certain textures on their feet – respect children's likes and dislikes.

Key words and gestures

- Use gestures and facial expressions to reinforce what you say: 'What does that feel like?' 'Is it wet, dry, cold, warm…?' 'Can you feel the sand between your toes?' 'Let's have a look' 'What's that?' 'Can you see the…?' 'Look at the colour, it's…' 'Can you feel it?' 'Does it feel… soft, hard, rough, smooth?' 'Do you like that?' 'Look at the pattern you have made' 'Footprints' 'What happens if…' 'Let's wash your feet and toes'.
- Maintain contact with the child to keep their attention.

Who am I?

This core activity is suitable for a small group of young children.

What you need:

A selection of clothing in a basket – hats, gloves, socks, sunglasses, wigs, shoes and coats

A quiet area in a corner

A mirror

A camera

Enhancing the activity

- Dress a teddy bear up in clothing, saying 'Find a hat and put the hat on teddy'.
- Make some simple masks.

Dressing up is fun and exciting for young children. This activity focuses on learning to follow instructions while exploring new and different textures and fabrics.

What you do

1 Sit comfortably on the floor with the basket of clothing in the middle.
2 Talk to the children about what's in the basket, naming and describing the items of clothing as you show them.
3 Let the children touch and explore the clothes.
4 Put all the clothes back in to the basket.
5 Ask each child in turn to find an article of clothing and put it on e.g. 'Sam, find a hat and put it on'.
6 Allow time for the child to follow the instruction.
7 Hold the mirror and show the child what they look like.
8 Repeat until all the children are wearing a number of different garments.
9 Use the mirror to keep showing the children what they look like.
10 Remember to dress up too!
11 Now reverse the game 'Sam take the hat off and put back in to the basket'.
12 If the children are still interested in the basket, let them explore the items by themselves.
13 Throughout the activity, take photographs of the children.

Extending the challenge

- Add a colour instruction: 'Find a red hat...'
- Match and sort by size, colour or pairs.
- Talk about the textures and fabrics of clothing.
- For older children
  - Give two instructions to follow 'Find a hat and some shoes...'
  - Include fastening and unfastening clothing.
  - Include clothing from around the world.
  - Sing any songs and rhymes with the children such as This is the way we...

Look, listen and note

Does the child...
* *Understand and follow simple instructions?*
* *Put on and take off clothes?*
* *Concentrate – how long until he/she responds?*
* *Do they enjoy dressing up and playing in role?*
* *Use recognisable words or put two words together to describe the clothes? e.g. Daddy's hat, my glasses.*

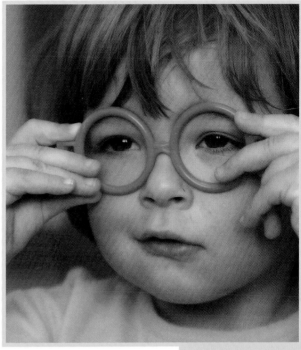

Take it outside

* This activity can easily be transferred to outside.
* Make a safe and dry place for children to sit and explore the basket of clothing.

Key words and gestures

* Use of the child's name
* Use gesture and facial expression to reinforce what you say: 'Are you ready?' 'Let's have some fun' 'Let's do some dressing up' 'Can you find...' 'Let's put it back in to the basket 'Let's look in the mirror' 'Does it fit you?' 'What colour is that?' 'Can you feel it? 'Is it soft, hard, fluffy...?' 'Can you say that?' 'Well done' 'Can you copy me?' 'What a good boy/girl you are!' 'Listen' 'Look'

TOP TIP
Be aware of the risks of certain items of clothing such as jewellery and ties.

Involving parents

You could...
* *Display some of the photographs you have taken of the activity to show parents.*
* *Ask parents to bring in any unwanted items of clothing to add to your basket.*
* *Share clothing from around the world.*

Parachute play

This core activity is suitable small group of young children from 24 months.

What you need:

A small parachute or piece of fabric

A soft toy

A large clear space

Extra adults

Enhancing the activity

- Use a ball for the game such as a beach ball, a table tennis ball or a 'koosh' ball.

♪ Sing a song about the toy parachute songs are few and far between!) Make one up if you can't remember one – or use a nursery rhyme or your own words to a familiar tune.

This activity encourages children to listen, follow instructions and become familiar with language through the use of repetition, whilst having fun with a parachute.

What you do

1 Clear a space indoors, which is big enough for you and the children to easily move about as you hold the edges of the parachute.
2 Give each child a handle to hold and pull the parachute tight, so it is taut. Another adult may be needed to help.
3 Gain the children's attention by saying their names.
4 Talk to the children about what you are going to do and give them a simple instruction: 'Hold the edge of the parachute Let's lift the parachute gently up and down'.
5 Allow time for the children to follow each instruction.
6 Use plenty of voice tone to exaggerate the movements of the parachute: 'It's going up' 'It's going down'.
7 Repeat this until the children have got used to the movement of the parachute.
8 Now place the soft toy in to the middle of the parachute and bounce the toy gently up and down: 'Look, Teddy is going up and down'.
9 Continue to play while the children are still interested.

Look, listen and note

Does the child…
- *Understand and follow simple instructions?*
- *Share, take turns, work with children or copy others?*
- *Concentrate? For how long?*
- *Use recognisable words?*
- *Enjoy working together?*

Key words and gestures

- Use of the child's name
- Use gesture and facial expression to reinforce what you say: 'Are you ready?' 'Let's have some fun' 'It's going up' 'It's going down' 'Up' 'Down' 'Quick' 'Slow' 'Fast' 'Can you say that?' 'Well done' 'Can you copy me?' 'What a good boy/girl you are!' 'Listen' 'Look'.
- Maintain contact with the child to keep their attention.

Involving parents

You could…
- Take some photos and display them, so parents can see how you do the activity.
- Have the activity out and show the parents how to do it at home, using a piece of old sheeting or a big scarf.

Take it outside

- This activity can easily be transferred to outside.
- Always check to be sure children are protected from the sun, from the damp and wind, from other children who may be playing nearby, and from insects and other wildlife.

Extending the challenge

- Up the challenge – work together to move the parachute more quickly or more slowly.
- Stretch the parachute tight and then release it.
- For older children
  - Use smaller items e.g. balls or soft toys.
  - Make a den and hide under the parachute.
  - Work with larger groups of children.

TOP TIP

A small piece of fabric will be more manageable with a smaller, younger group of children.

Matching pictures

This core activity is suitable for one child.

What you need:

Pictures and photographs of everyday objects

Matching objects for each of the pictures

A shoe box

A quiet and undisrupted area

A blanket

Enhancing the activity

- Increase the number of objects in the box.
- Take photographs of children's own items e.g. a favourite toy or clothing and match these.

♪ Sing a song about the pictures. Make it up if you can't remember one or use a nursery rhyme or your own words to a familiar tune.

This activity is a great way of introducing new words, and by using repetition you will encourage the children to recognise and match the words to actual objects that they can touch and explore.

What you do

1 Put three everyday objects, such as a book, a bunch of keys and a toy car in the shoebox and put the lid on.
2 Shake the box and give it to the child to explore.
3 Show a picture of one of the objects and ask the child to find the object in the box: 'Look, it's a...' 'Can you find one the same?'
4 Allow time for the child to find the object by themselves.
5 Hold the picture and the object together and say: 'Well done, look they are the same'.
6 Play on, matching more objects and pictures.
7 Encourage the child to identify the pictures and objects by themselves.
8 Use plenty of praise and encouragement.
9 Continue the activity while the child is still interested.

Key words and gestures

- Use of the child's name
- Use gesture and facial expression to reinforce what you say: 'Are you ready?' 'What is that?' 'It's a...' 'Can you find one the same?' 'What does it look like?' 'How does that feel?' 'Well done, it's the same' 'They match' 'Can you do that again?' 'Look in the box' 'What can you hear?' 'It sounds like...' 'Listen' 'Look'
- Maintain contact with the child to keep their attention.

Take it outside

- This activity can easily be transferred outside by placing a blanket and cushions under a tree.
- Have photographs and items from the outside environment e.g. leaves, soil, twigs and flowers.

Look, listen and note

Does the child…
- *Understand and follow simple instructions?*
- *Sort and match?*
- *Recognise objects?*
- *Concentrate? For how long?*
- *Use recognisable words?*
- *Enjoy the activity?*

Extending the challenge

- Look out for simple photo picture books and match objects to these pictures.
- Match textures and fabrics e.g. sand paper, fur or foil.
- For older children:
    - Try matching pictures to pictures.
    - Cover a tray with pictures and give the children a box of objects that match the pictures.
    - Play picture pairs.

TOP TIP
You don't have to use a camera, be creative and use pictures from magazines, old books and catalogues to match to objects.

Involving parents

You could…
- *Take some photos and display them, so parents can see how you do the activity.*
- *Have the activity out and show the parents how to do it at home. Take photographs of favourite items/family members and use these to make loan packs.*
- *Match the child's item to another family members item e.g. Daddy's toothbrush, your toothbrush.*

Row, row, row your boat

This core activity is suitable for a small group of young children.

What you need:

An adult for each child

A blanket

A quiet uninterrupted space

Enhancing the activity

- Include a teddy bear in your game. Hold the teddy in front of your body so they can be included.

♪ Sing other songs and rhymes such as *See-saw Margery Daw*, *Ring a ring of roses* or *The Grand Old Duke of York*.

Take it outside

- Nursery rhymes and action songs are easily transferred to an outside area.
- Always check to be sure children are protected from the sun when playing games and singing songs out of doors. Sing songs associated with outdoors, such as Two little dickie birds.

Row, row, row your boat is a lovely action song that enables you to face the child directly whilst singing.

What you do

1 Place the blanket in a safe, warm area, preferably without any draughts. Make sure there is enough room to move freely without any obstacles in the way.
2 The adults sit on the blanket, each with a child between their legs, facing each other, and holding both hands.
3 Gently say the child's name to get their attention.
4 Talk to the child and ask: 'Shall we sing Row, row, row your boat?'
5 As you start to sing the song, gently rock backwards and forwards making sure the child is fully supported and feels safe.
6 Use plenty of facial expression and make sure you smile during the song!
7 Maintain eye contact with the child and watch their reaction carefully.
8 Use a range of voice tones to keep them interested.
9 Sing the song again, repeating the first verse, or using a different verse of the action song.
10 When you think the child has had enough, pick his/her up and give them a hug.

Look, listen and note

Does the child...
- *Use a range of language such as describing words, object words, action words and prepositions?*
- *Interact with other children? Does he/she imitate and copy, take turns and share?*
- *Stay engaged? For how long?*
- *Enjoy the activity?*
- *Follow instructions and making decisions?*

Key words and gestures

- Use of the child's name
- Use gesture and facial expression to reinforce what you say: 'Shall we do some singing?' 'Are you ready?' 'Let's sing quietly' 'Soft' 'Loud' 'Let's do it again' 'Did you enjoy that?' 'What a clever boy/girl you are' 'Can you hear me?' 'Can you do it?' 'Look' 'Listen' 'Let's...' 'Backwards' 'Forwards' 'Sideways' 'Quickly' 'Slowly'
- Use eye contact and touch to keep the child focused and attentive.

Extending the challenge

- Sing the song loudly or quietly using a range of voice tones.
- Up the tempo and sing the song more quickly. Be careful not to jerk the child's head or arms.
- For older children
    - Two children can play on their own, with your support, if needed.
    - Move sideways instead of backwards and forwards.
    - Encourage the children to choose another action songs they want to sing.
    - Just observe the children and encourage them to take the lead – don't join in yourself.

Involving parents

You could...
- *Use an action rhyme booklet made especially for parents to enjoy at home.*
- *Photographs and displays can help parents to see their children having fun and enjoying songs and simple rhymes.*

TOP TIP
Make sure there is enough room to be able move freely without any obstacles getting in the way.

Ribbon sticks

This core activity is suitable for a small group of young children from 16 months.

What you need:

A selection of ribbon sticks

A large enough space to move about

A blanket

Enhancing the activity

- Add bells to the ribbon sticks
- Provide a selection of dressing up clothes for the children to use

♪ Instead of using music, sing a selection of rhymes for the children to move to such as: *This is the way we dance, The Grand Old Duke Of York, Oranges and Lemons* or *Here we go round the Mulberry bush.*

TOP TIP
Make sure you have plenty of space to move freely about with the ribbon sticks.

Using ribbon sticks is a very visual way of maintaining children's interest, extending their physical experiences as they sing and dance. Ribbon sticks are easy to make and children will love using them. SF – will practitioners make the link between this and early phonics?? Need to point this out?

What you do

1 Sit together on the blanket.
2 Put a selection of ribbons sticks n the middle of the blanket and show the children each stick, describing the colours of the ribbons.
3 Show the children different ways of using the sticks, up and down, round and round or shaking and wafting.
4 Encourage the children to watch and listen carefully to the sounds and movements the ribbons make.
5 Allow the children to choose which ribbon stick they want to use – encourage 'please' and 'thank you'.
6 Put on some music and dance around with the sticks to the rhythm and the beat of the music.
7 Change the music and offer different types and styles of music to encourage different types of movement.
8 Allow the children to swap the ribbon sticks and make sure you join in too!

Extending the challenge

- Use a selection of fabrics such as chiffon scarves sari fabric or small blankets
- Talk about the textures of the materials
- For older children
  - Encourage the children to make their own ribbon sticks.
  - Make one large ribbon stick with two sticks for two children to use together.
  - Allow the children to choose the music for the dance.

Look, listen and note

Does the child...

- *Use a range of language such as describing words, object words, action words and prepositions?*
- *Interact with other children, copying, taking turns and sharing?*
- *Show an ability to express themselves through dance and music?*
- *Enjoy the activity?*
- *Stay engaged? For how long?*

Key words and gestures

- Use of the children's names
- Use gesture and facial expression to reinforce what you say: 'Shall we do some dancing?' 'Are you ready?' 'Which one do you want?' 'Let's do it again' 'Did you enjoy that?' 'Can you hear me?' 'Can you do it?' 'Look' 'Listen' 'Let's...'
- Use different voice tones to keep their attention.

Take it outside

- Ribbon sticks are easily used outside and are perfect on a windy day.
- Follow your health and safety policy when taking electrical items outside such as a CD player
- Always check to be sure children are protected from the sun, from the damp and wind, from other children who may be playing nearby, and from insects or other wildlife.
- Sing songs associated with outdoors such as *Two little dickie birds.*

Involving parents

You could...

- *Display the ribbon sticks attractively along with photographs of the children using them, to show parents the enjoyment of this activity.*
- *Display a range of suitable music with different beats and rhythms for simple dance activities.*

Rhythm time!

This core activity is suitable for a small group of young children.

What you need:

A selection of household items such as saucepans, wooden and metal spoons, a bunch of keys, a box, containers, plastic bowls, washing up brushes etc

A blanket

A warm safe area

Enhancing the activity

- Sing songs while making sounds.
- Play the items quickly and slowly.

♪ Sing any songs or use a nursery rhyme or your own words to a familiar tune such as *I am the music man, I can play on the big bass drum* or *This is the way we...*

Household items are very versatile resources and are a great way for young children of all ages to explore and enjoy a range of textures and materials. They can be used in a variety of ways to stimulate and engage children through rhythm and beat as their language develops.

What you do

1. Think carefully about safety when choosing household items.
2. Spread the blanket in a safe, warm place.
3. Sit with the children in front of you.
4. Introduce each household item and place it on the floor between you and the children.
5. Pick up an item, say what it is and make a sound with it, by either moving it, tapping it on the floor or taping two items together.
6. Watch the children's responses.
7. When the children reach out, hand over the item for them to touch and handle, talking as you do so: 'Do you want the saucepan and spoon? Here you go'.
8. Smile as you talk, maintaining eye contact.
9. Let the children experiment with the sounds and explore the items.
10. You hold an item and play along, introducing different rhythms and beats.
11. Encourage the children to watch, to listen to you and to copy you.
12. When interest flags, change the items around and let the children explore something different.

Extending the challenge

- Encourage the children to listen to you and take turns.
- Play quietly and loudly.
- Track the sounds: play an item behind, above or at the side of the children.
- For older children:
  - Play a range of music in the background. Can the children tap to the beat?
  - Can they stop when you ask them to?
  - Experiment with sounds. What happens if we change a wooden spoon to a metal spoon?
  - Recognise the sounds: hide and play the items out of sight of the children and see if they can identify them.

Look, listen and note

Does the child…
- *Follow the movements and sounds (tracking)?*
- *Use a range of language?*
- *Follow simple instructions?*
- *Interact with other children, copying, taking turns and sharing?*
- *Smile and use other body movements to show enjoyment?*
- *Concentrate? For how long?*

Key words and gestures

- Use of the children's name
- Names of sounds
- Repeated sound and rhythmical phrases help children language to develop – use 'tap, tap, tap' or 'bang' 'bang' 'bang' to accompany their sound patterns.
- Use gesture and facial expression to reinforce what you say: 'What can you see?' 'Look it's a…' 'Can you hear the…?' 'What a lovely noise it makes' 'Shall we sing a song?' 'Did you enjoy that?' 'That was lovely' 'Tap loudly, quietly, noisily' 'Beat' 'Rhythm' 'Listen' 'Hush' 'Let's take turns' 'Can you stop?'

Involving parents

You could…
- *Collect and display some suitable everyday objects to use.*
- *Encourage parents to experiment with household music in the kitchen or at bath time.*

Take it outside

- A great activity to take outside and make lots of noise!
- Go around the garden and make different sounds such as tapping on a tree trunk, running a stick along a fence or scraping a fork on a grating or drainpipe.
- Always check to be sure children are safe and supervised when using objects on the move.

TOP TIP
Be aware of the safety issues when using household items.

Ring-a-ring-of-roses

This core activity is suitable for a small group of young children.

Ring games are a great way of communicating with young children as you all have fun singing and dancing. Start with familiar ones and old favourites.

Enhancing the activity

- Use a selection of toy fishes to have in the middle of the circle for when you sing the second verse – '...fishes in the water'.

♪ There are many action songs that can be used to sing in a circle – here are just a few: *Five little men in a flying saucer, Little sandy girl, The farmer's in his den, Alice the camel* and *The Hokey kokey.*

Involving parents

You could...
- *Develop an action rhyme booklet for parents to use at home.*
- *Encourage parents to tell you about their favourite rhymes and add these to your collection.*

What you do

1   Talk to the children about the ring games you are about to do, as you get ready to go outside. Use an excited voice to gain their interest: 'Are we ready?' 'Let's go and have some fun outside playing Ring-a-ring-of-roses'.
2   Find an area outside, big enough to allow you to move freely. Remove any toys or obstructions out of the way.
3   Form a circle with the children, holding hands and all facing inwards. If you have an unconfident child you may want to stand next to them, so they can hold an adult's hand for support and reassurance.
4   Call out the child's name to gain their attention saying '... are you ready?'
5   Start to sing the rhyme and as you do so, slowly walk around in a circle. Use a nursery rhyme book for guidance on these actions if needed.
6   Use plenty of facial expressions and voice tone as you sing.
7   As you 'all fall down', gently do the actions to the song using exaggerated movements for the children to copy.
8   Praise the children for joining in and offer support and extra reassurance for children who are not so confident.
9   While the children are enjoying themselves, repeat the rhyme.

Take it inside

- These action songs are easily transferred to inside but remember there must be enough room to move freely about. You may need to clear away furniture and toys to ensure the children do not trip and fall over any obstacles
- Be aware of the noise levels you may make – are you disturbing anyone?

TOP TIP
Remember not all children are confident so may need support and reassurance during lively action songs.

Look, listen and note

Does the child...
- *Use a range of language such as describing words, object words, action words and prepositions?*
- *Interact with other children, copying, taking turns and sharing?*
- *Stay engaged? For how long?*
- *Have fun?*
- *Follow instructions and make decisions?*

Key words and gestures

- Use of the children's names.
- Use gesture and facial expression to reinforce what you say: 'Shall we do some singing?' 'Are you ready?' 'Let's sing quietly' 'Softy' 'Loudly' 'Let's do it again' 'Did you enjoy that?' 'What a clever boy/girl you are' 'Can you hear me?' 'Can you do it?' 'Look' 'Listen' 'Let's...' 'Which song shall we sing now?' 'Shall we do it together?' 'Well done' 'Let's change directions' 'Backwards, forwards'.
- Maintain contact with the children and use different voice tones to keep their attention.

Extending the challenge

- Use different voice tones – sing quietly, loudly or whisper.
- For older children:
  - Encourage the children to choose which songs they want to sing next.
  - Up the tempo and move quickly during the rhyme. Change directions.
  - Sometimes, just observe the children and encourage them to take the lead – don't join in yourself.

I play, you play

This core activity is suitable for a small group of young children.

Enhancing the activity

* Try playing 'Play and stop'. Encourage the children to follow your simple instructions and stop on a simple hand signal.

♪ Sing songs such as *I am the music man*, *This is the way we play our instruments*, *I can play on the shaker* and *this is the way I do it*.

'I play, you play' is a fun activity which encourages children to take turns and to respond when using a range of musical instruments.

What you do

1. Place the blanket in a safe, warm area, preferably without any drafts. Make sure there is enough room to move freely without any obstacles in the way.
2. Sit on the blanket with the children next to you.
3. Call the children's names individually to get their attention.
4. Put the sound makers on the floor between you and let the children point and choose one each.
5. As you give them the instrument, say its name.
6. Choose one for yourself.
7. Let the children experiment with the sound makers.
8. Now play 'I play, you play'. You play first. They play in response.
9. Encourage the children to listen to you and take turns.
10. They may find this difficult to start with so offer lots of praise and encouragement.
11. Use plenty of facial expressions and smile during the activity!
12. Repeat while the children are interested.

Extending the challenge

* Let the children play first and you copy in turn.
* For older children:
  * Use different instructions ¬– 'I play quickly, you play quickly'.
  * Use a simple sound maker at story time. Play the sound maker each time a character appears or you want the children to move.
  * Let the children make their own sound makers e.g. with plastic bottles and pasta.

TOP TIP
Use a quiet area where there will be minimum distractions and the children will be able to hear your instructions.

Key words and gestures

* Use of the child's name
* Use gesture and facial expression to reinforce what you say: 'What have we got?' 'Look' 'Are you ready?' 'Let's play our sound makers...quietly, softly, loudly' 'Let's do it again' 'Did you enjoy that?' 'Can you do that?'
* Maintain contact with the child and use different voice tones to keep their attention.

Look, listen and note

Does the child...
- *Use a range of language and understand the words?*
- *Interact with other children, copying, taking turns and sharing?*
- *Stay engaged? For how long?*
- *Enjoy the activity?*
- *Follow instructions, including signals to stop and start.*

Take it outside

- This activity is easily transferred to outside.
- Place a blanket under a tree for children to enjoy the activity outside.
- Listen out for sounds in the garden.
- Always check to be sure children are protected from the sun and other children who may be playing more boisterous games.

Involving parents

You could...
- *Make simple sound makers for parents to take home and use with their children.*
- *Provide some simple song and rhyme books or CDs of nursery rhymes.*
- *Take photographs and display for parents so they can see their children having fun with simple music making.*

Teddy bears' picnic

This core activity is suitable for a small group of young children from 16 months.

What you need:

A large picnic blanket

A large space outside

A selection of Teddy bears

A picnic

A dry day!

Enhancing the activity

- Use different voice tone – sing quietly, loudly or whisper.

♪ Sing songs about what you have seen. If you can't remember one, make up a song or have a songbook to hand to look at. Try: *Round and round the garden* or *Teddy bear, Teddy bear, touch your nose.*

With a little imagination, many rhymes and songs come alive for children. This classic song is a perfect example by adding role-play resources or using toys to play out the rhymes.

What you do

1 Ask the parents to bring in a Teddy bear for their child from home.
2 Have a selection of spare bears available so all the children have one and you have one too!
3 Take the group of children outside with their bears and sit them on the picnic blanket.
4 Set out the picnic things where the children can see them and talk about them.
5 As the children eat their picnic, softly start to sing Teddy bears' picnic.
6 Use plenty of facial expressions and voice tone as you sing. Use a nursery rhyme book or a CD player to help if you need it.
7 Praise the children for joining in asking them if they and their Teddy bears are having fun.
8 While the children are enjoying themselves, repeat the rhyme.

Extending the challenge

- Decorate the paper plates for the picnic.
- Make Teddy bear face masks or Teddy bears figures on sticks.
- For older children:
  - Make the picnic with the children e.g. sandwiches, cakes, vegetable sticks and dips etc.
  - Go to the local park and have the teddy bears picnic there.

Look, listen and note

Does the child...
- *Use a range of language such as describing words, object words, action words and prepositions?*
- *Follow instructions and make decisions?*
- *Interact with other children, copying, taking turns and sharing?*
- *Enjoy this event and bring their own toy from home?*
- *Stay engaged? For how long?*

Take it inside

- 'Teddy bears' picnic' is easily transferred to inside but remember there must be enough room for your picnic. You may need to clear away furniture and toys to ensure the children don't trip and fall over any obstacles.
- Be aware of the noise levels – are you disturbing anyone?

Involving parents

You could...
- *Bring in their child's Teddy bear and join the picnic.*
- *Display photographs for the parents to see the 'Teddy bears' picnic'.*

Key words and gestures

- Use of the children's name.
- Use gesture and facial expression to reinforce what you say: 'Shall we go on a picnic?' 'Are you ready?' 'Let's go outside' 'Have you got your Teddy bear?' 'Let's sing...quietly, softly, loudly' 'Let's do it again' 'What do you want to eat?' 'Let's eat...' 'Did you enjoy that?' 'Can you do it?' 'Look' 'Listen' 'Let's...'
- Maintain contact with the children and use different voice tones to keep their attention.

TOP TIP
Most children love Teddy bears, but be aware, there may be a child who is frightened.

Wind the bobbin up

This core activity is suitable for a small group of young children.

What you need:

A blanket

A quiet uninterrupted space

At least one adult

Enhancing the activity

- Use different voice tone – sing quietly, loudly or whisper.
- Have a large doll, Teddy or puppet in your lap and help them to make the movements. Big puppets with glove hands are especially good for this.

♪ Sing songs about what you have seen. If you can't remember one, make up a song or have a songbook at hand to look at. Familiar tunes such as these can be used with your own words: *Row, row, row your boat*, *Tommy Thumb* or *Five little ducks*

Nursery rhymes are a great way of communicating with babies, and songs with actions are particularly good for developing language. 'Wind the bobbin up' is a simple action rhyme perfect for singing and playing with very young children.

What you do

1 Sit yourselves comfortably on the blanket with the children facing you.
2 Talk to the children about the singing time and introduce this rhyme: 'Shall we sing wind the bobbin up?'
3 Softly start to sing the rhyme.
4 Use plenty of facial expressions and voice tone as you sing.
5 Gently do the actions to the song using exaggerated movements for the children to copy. Put a nursery rhyme book on the floor nearby for guidance on these actions if you need it.
6 Praise the children for joining in and offer support and extra reassurance for children who are not so confident. You may find it useful to have more than one adult involved so all the children can be helped to join in.
7 While the children are enjoying themselves, repeat the rhyme or introduce a different one.

Extending the challenge

- Change the end to include the children's name or various body parts '... and lay them on ....'s shoulder'.
- For older children:
  - Encourage the children to choose which songs they want to sing.
  - Introduce musical instruments, so some children can accompany while the others do the movements.

TOP TIP
Keep introducing and repeating new rhymes and songs to young children, but don't forget old favourites!

Look, listen and note

Does the child…
- *Use a range of language such as describing words, object words, action words and prepositions?*
- *Interact with other children, copying, taking turns and sharing?*
- *Join in (individually) with the singing, the movements or both?*
- *Follow your lead?*
- *Stay engaged? For how long?*

Take it outside

- Nursery rhymes and action songs are easily transferred to the garden where you can make more noise and do bigger movements.
- Always check to be sure children are protected from the sun when you do singing sessions outdoors.
- Sing songs associated with being outdoors, such as *Two little dickie birds*.

Key words and gestures

- Use of the children's name
- Use gesture and facial expression to reinforce what you say: 'Shall we do some singing?' 'Are you ready?' 'Let's sing… quietly, softly, loudly.' 'Let's do it again' 'Did you enjoy that?' 'You joined in well' 'Can you hear me?' 'Can you do it?' 'Look' 'Listen' 'Let's…'
- Maintain eye contact with the children and use different voice tones to keep their attention.

Involving parents

You could…
- *Parents might like to have a copy of a booklet of action songs and rhymes to use at home.*
- *Encourage parents to use every day occurrences to sing to their child – nappy time, trips in the car or in the supermarket queue.*

A quiet time activity

This core activity is suitable for one child or a small group of young children.

What you need:

An assortment of soft, floor cushions

A quiet uninterrupted space, preferably in a corner

A range of good quality books – picture, words, board and story books

Storage baskets or units

Enhancing the activity

• Have quiet soothing music on in the background.
• To keep the quiet area interesting change the books frequently and also check their condition.

♪ Sing any quiet songs or use a nursery rhyme of your own words to a familiar tune such as *Hush a bye baby* or *Miss Polly had a dolly*.

During the day all children will need the opportunity to have a quiet time, either by themselves or with a familiar adult or friends. This activity is ideal for a quiet area full of interesting and exciting books.

What you do

1 Find a corner area that is uninterrupted and quiet.
2 Place all the cushions attractively within the area both on the floor and up against the walls.
3 Put a selection of books in the basket and place it between the cushions.
4 Take a few of the books out of the basket and stand them up or put them on the cushions.
5 Observe your group, and when a child goes into the quiet book area, watch what they do. Are they looking at books and telling themselves a story? If they are happy and involved on their own, don't interrupt!
6 If you think the child would welcome your presence, offer to read to the child. Encourage the child to choose the book, by saying 'Which book would you like?'
7 Sit on the cushions with the child and quietly look at the book together. They may want a cuddle during the story or a favourite toy to hold.
8 Other children will often join you as soon as they see you reading, so include them too.
9 Maintain contact with the child or the small group, and observe them for their reactions. A child may just want to be on their own, so you need to manage additional children carefully, or get help from another adult.
10 When finished, encourage the child to put the book back and if still content, choose another story together.

Take it outside

• Books are easily transferred to outside areas and provide another activity to tempt children into the fresh air.
• Place a blanket under a tree or in a quieter area of your outside area, with a basket full of books.
• Put some books near the outside door, with little bags or baskets so children can take a favourite story out of doors.
• Read books associated with outdoors, such as *We're Going on a Bear Hunt* and sing *Round and round the garden* or *Here we go round the Mulberry bush*.

Look, listen and note

Does the child...
- *Use a range of language such as describing words, object words, action words, prepositions?*
- *Interact with other children, copying, taking turns, sharing stories and 'reading' to each other or to soft toys?*
- *Stay engaged? For how long?*
- *Enjoy books and stories on their own?*
- *Make decisions about stories to read or share?*

Key words and gestures

- Use of the child's name
- Use gesture and facial expression to reinforce what you say: 'Shall we have a look at a book?' 'Do you want to choose one?' 'Which one?' 'Is that the book you want?' 'Are you ready?' 'Let's read quietly' 'Let's begin' 'Let's do it again' 'Did you enjoy that?' 'What a clever boy/girl you are!' 'Can you put the book back for me?' 'Look' 'Listen' 'Let's...'
- If you are working with an individual, maintain physical contact with the child and use different voice tones to keep their attention.

Involving parents

You could...
- *Make a book list of favourite books for parents to have at home.*
- *Take their children to the local library or use 'Book Start' programmes.*

Extending the challenge

- Use story aids to enhance the story.
- For older children:
  - Just observe the children and encourage them to take the lead. Who would like to read a book?
  - Make your own storybooks.
  - Visit a library and bring back some extra books or read a story in the library.

TOP TIP

Make sure the books are in good condition and appeal to the children's current interests.

Our very own books!

This core activity is suitable for one or a small group of children from 24 months.

What you need:

A selection of mark making materials and equipment such as pens, pencils, felt tips and crayons

Large pieces of card

A laminator (optional)

Treasury tags

Floor cushions

A story for a stimulus, such as *The Very Hungry Caterpillar* by Eric Carle

Enhancing the activity

- Have paint available for the illustrations.
- Have The Very Hungry Caterpillar story sack available for children to look at before they start on their own versions.

♪ Link songs and rhymes to the book such as: *There's a very furry caterpillar*, *Little Arabella Miller*, *I've got a basket of apples* and *Old MacDonald had a shop*.

All children love books and this activity will provide them with the opportunity to work with each other to create and make their own book.

What you do

1 After a story session, sit with the children and ask them if they would like to make their own book.
2 Use your voice and facial expression to provoke interest and to encourage children to join in the exciting activity of making their own books.
3 Talk to the children about the book they want to make: 'Would you like to make our very own Hungry Caterpillar book?'
4 Show the children the actual book. If possible, have more than one copy of the book available.
5 Allow the children to choose which page of the story they want to create. It doesn't matter if more than one child wants to make the same page.
6 Provide enough time for the children to create their own pages for the book, encouraging them to choose which mark making materials they want to use, and helping them if they need it.
7 Use plenty of praise and encouragement with the children and observe their response.
8 When all the children have finished, collect the pages and laminate each one. Then hole punch and tie together with treasury tags.
9 Sit together on some comfortable cushions and look at your very own The Very Hungry Caterpillar book.
10 At the end of the story, praise all the children for creating such a special book.
11 Keep the book in the book corner and plan for more book making sessions.

Take it outside

- This activity can be taken outside on a warm day, but avoid the rain and wind!
- Make a textured book using natural items found in the garden or photos.
- Always check children are protected from the sun when doing static activities outside on a sunny day.

TOP TIP
If using a laminator, remember they get very hot!

Look, listen and note

Does the child...
- *Use a range of language such as describing words, object words, action words and prepositions?*
- *Interact with other children, copying, working together, taking turns and sharing?*
- *Show an ability to express themselves through mark making?*
- *Enjoy the process and the finished book?*
- *Stay engaged? For how long?*

Involving parents

You could...
- *Display the books attractively with photos of the children making the book to show parents the scope of this activity.*
- *Encourage parents to bring in photos of the children's family to make a 'My Family Book'.*

Key words and gestures

- Use of the children's name
- Use gesture and facial expression to reinforce what you say: 'Shall we make our own book?' 'How exciting is this?' 'Are you ready?' 'Which one do you want?' 'Can you tell the story?' 'Well done, I'm so proud of you' 'Shall we show...?' 'Let's do it again' 'Did you enjoy that?' 'Can you do it?' 'Look' 'Listen' "Let's..."

Extending the challenge

- Encourage the children to choose which storybook they want to make.
- Take photographs of all the children and make a book of 'Ourselves'.
- For older children:
  - Encourage the children to write words and do 'have-a-go' writing.
  - Role-play the story before you make a book. 'Whole body' story telling is a very good way of learning the story.
  - Encourage the children to make up their own stories for books.

Prop boxes and bags

This core activity is suitable for a small group of children from 20 months.

What you need:

A drawstring bag or a container

The Tiger Who Came To Tea by Judith Kerr, or a book of your own choice

A soft tiger

A selection of play food and drink

A tin labelled Tiger Food

A quiet book area with large comfortable floor cushions

Enhancing the activity

- Add a photograph of a tiger in its natural habitat.
- Encourage the children to listen to you and take turns with the props.

♪ Sing any songs or use a nursery rhyme or your own words to a familiar tune such as *Walking through the jungle* or *Down in the jungle*.

Prop boxes or story bags are a great resource and will enhance any storybook. With a bit of imagination, you can easily collect items related to a specific book and then during the story session, use the visuals to bring the book alive whilst introducing new words and vocabulary!

What you do

1 Collect all the props needed and make your own *The Tiger Who Came To Tea* prop bag.
2 Sit comfortably in the book area with a small group of children.
3 Gain the children's interest by telling the story *The Tiger Who Came To Tea*.
4 After the story, introduce the prop bag to the children. Shake it, let the children touch the outside and ask them if they can guess what's inside.
5 Take out one item and show it to the children, saying 'Look it's the Tiger and he has come for some tea'. Pass the Tiger round and let the children explore it at their own pace.
6 Now take out the other items from the bag and look at these together.
7 Watch the children's responses.
8 Put all the items back in the prop bag and tell the story again, but this time use the props as you do so.
9 Let the children hold the items after you have used them for the story.
10 At the end of the story, allow time for the children to explore both the book and the props.
11 At the end of the session, put the items back in the prop bag and finish the session with 'What a lovely story that was, did you enjoy it?'

Extending the challenge

- Make story bags for other favourite stories and leave them in the book corner for children to use independently.
- Use dough to make and bake your own food to use as a story aid.
- Ask the children to guess the next prop that will come out of the bag.
- For older children:
  - Have labels in the prop bag – 'tiger, food, tea, drink...'
  - Let the children tell the story by themselves using the props.
  - Make a The Tiger Who Came To Tea or Monkey Puzzle book and a bag of objects to go with it.

Look, listen and note

Does the child...
* *Use a range of language?*
* *Follow simple instructions?*
* *Interact with other children, copying, taking turns, sharing, 'reading' or telling their own stories?*
* *Anticipate what's going to happen next?*
* *Show enjoyment?*
* *Concentrate for long?*

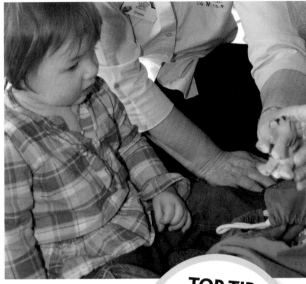

TOP TIP

Prop bags don't have to be expensive, look around and you will be amazed at the everyday objects that can be linked to a storybook!

Key words and gestures

* Use of the children's name
* Names of sounds
* Repeated sound and rhythmical phrases help children's language to develop.
* Use gesture and facial expression to reinforce what you say: 'Shall we choose a book?' 'Which one do you want?' 'What can you see?' 'Can you guess what's in the bag?' 'Look it's a...' 'Can you tell the story?' 'Are we ready?' 'Let's begin' 'What's that?' 'Did you enjoy that?'

Take it outside

* Prop bags can be taken outside on a warm day. Place a blanket under a tree with some cushions to make the perfect quiet book area.
* Use the outdoor space to include larger items for props e.g. an empty cardboard box for the 'fridge'.
* Always check that children are protected from the sun when they sit for periods of time out of doors in sunny weather.

Involving parents

You could...
* *Display the prop bag alongside the book to show parents the activity.*
* *Encourage the parents to borrow prop bags to use at home with the children.*

Let's pretend!

This core activity is suitable for a small group of children from 24 months.

Enhancing the activity

- Make some face masks for each character.

- ♪ There are many action songs that can be sung – here are just a few: *Dingle, dangle scarecrow, One potato, two potato* or *This is the way we grow our turnips*

All children will have their favourite books, ones they want to look at again and again by themselves, with their peers and with you. Extend the value of every book through role-play.

What you do

1. Find an area big enough to allow you to move freely and remove any toys or objects out of the way to make a large area.
2. Sit on the cushions with the group of children and read *The Enormous Turnip* story.
3. After the story, use an excited voice to maintain their interest: 'Shall we have some fun playing The Enormous Turnip?'
4. Pass the turnip round so the children can feel it and look at it closely.
5. Put the turnip on the floor. Start to read the story again and as you turn each page, invite a child to stand up and be that character.
6. During the verse, use plenty of voice tone and facial expression to encourage the children to join in 'They pulled and pulled...'
7. Keep reading the book, allowing all the children to participate in the story. All the children will end up standing in a line, holding on to the child in front of them trying to pull the enormous turnip.
8. If you have a large group of children, add on extra characters so all the children are involved and 'pulling'.
9. At the end of the story, encourage the children to pull the turnip up and to gently all fall down, laughing with the fun and excitement!
10. Praise the children for joining in and offer support and extra reassurance for children who are not so confident.
11. While the children are enjoying themselves, they will probably want to repeat the story.

Extending the challenge

- Cook the turnip and have a tasting session.
- Choose another storybook to act out, such as *The Very busy Spider* by Eric Carle, *The Enormous Pancake* or *Follow My Leader* by Emma Chichester Clarke.
- Turn your home corner into a fruit and vegetable shop and make your own food to sell.
- For older children:
  - Grow your own turnips and other vegetables
  - Make a group book of *The Enormous Turnip* book
  - Just observe the children and encourage them to take the lead with the book – don't join in yourself.

Look, listen and note

Does the child...
* *Use a range of language such as describing words, object words, action words and prepositions?*
* *Interact with other children, copying, taking turns, sharing, working together and anticipating?*
* *Follow instructions and make decisions?*

Key words and gestures

* Use of the children's name
* Use gesture and facial expression to reinforce what you say: 'Shall we choose a book?' 'Let's have some fun' 'Are we ready?' 'Let's begin' 'Which one do you want?' 'What can you see?' 'Who wants to be the...' 'What happens next?' 'Can you guess what's...?' 'Look it's a ...' 'Can you tell the story?' 'What's that?' 'Did you enjoy that?' 'Pull, pull' 'Enormous' 'Vegetable'.
* Use different voices for the characters.

Take it outside

* Place a blanket under a tree with some cushions to make the perfect book area.
* Use the outdoor space to include larger items for props such as empty cardboard boxes, Wellington boots, dressing up clothes for the characters or hats, tails and masks to suit the story.
* Act out the story in your vegetable plot. Have Wellington boots and protective clothing available.

TOP TIP
Remember not all children are confident so may need support and reassurance during role play.

Involving parents

You could...
* Take photographs and display them for parents to see how much fun it is for their children and how the excitement of a book can be extended.
* Share information with parents on local libraries and 'Book Start'.
* Develop a list of suitable books for parents to have at home.

On the washing line

This core activity is suitable for a small group of children from 20 months.

What you need:

A washing line at the children's height

Wooden pegs (push-on or clip-on) in a basket

An old copy of a story book with a strong story line, such as *Whatever Next* by Jill Murphy

A newer copy of the book you using

A basket

A laminator

Large floor cushions or a rug

Enhancing the activity

- Colour or number the pegs.
- Use washing lines for sorting and counting activities.

♪ Sing songs about the book. If you can't remember one, make up a song or have a songbook to hand to look at. Try *Five little men in a flying saucer* or *Teddy bear, Teddy bear*.

Children love washing lines and pegs. This activity will encourage children to tell a favourite story by sequencing the pictures on the washing line and having the freedom to be creative with the order of the book!

What you do

1 When you have a book that is old, perhaps ripped and seen better days, don't throw it away, keep it and re-use it for this activity.
2 Pull the book apart and separately laminate each picture page. Place the pictures in a basket.
3 Sit with the children on the cushions and read the story from the new copy of the book.
4 After the story, use an excited voice to maintain their interest: 'Now shall we have some fun with the washing line?'
5 Encourage the children to look at each picture and peg the pictures on the washing line.
6 Talk about the beginning of the story and see if the children can sequence the pictures on the line.
7 Use the storybook to show the children and to help with the sequencing.
8 Offer lots of praise and encouragement.
9 Read the story again, matching the story to the washing line – does it match?
10 While the children are still enjoying themselves read the story again.

Take it outside

- Books and washing lines can easily be transferred outside but make sure you put them somewhere safe from children who are running about.
- Place a blanket under a tree with some cushions to make the perfect book area with the washing line next to it.
- Use the outdoor space to include larger items for props such as an empty cardboard box for the 'rocket', and act out the story (SF – which story?). Add some Wellington boots, sieves, food and some soft toys such as a Teddy bear and an owl.

Look, listen and note

Does the child…
- *Use a range of language such as describing words, object words, action words and prepositions?*
- *Follow instructions and make decisions?*
- *Anticipate what's going to happen next?*
- *Interact with other children, copying, taking turns and sharing?*
- *Understand the sequence and have the ability to follow this?*
- *Stay engaged – for how long?*

Involving parents

You could…
- Take photographs and display so parents can see how much fun their children are having and the value of washing lines and books.
- Encourage children to help with the pegging out of washing at home.

Key words and gestures

- Use of the children's name
- Use gesture and facial expression to reinforce what you say: 'Let's look at the book' 'Are you ready?' 'What comes first?' 'Let's start at the beginning' 'What do you think?' 'Where is that?' 'Can you match?' 'Is it the same?' 'Can you do that?' 'Let's put that on the line' 'Can you do it?' 'Look' 'Listen' 'Let's…'
- Stay with the children as they work and use different voice tones to keep their attention.

Extending the challenge

- Talk about the beginning, the middle and the end of the book.
- Sequence another book, such as *We're Going On A Bear Hunt*.
- For older children:
    - Make a 'My Day' washing line. Take photographs at different times of the children's day, laminate and then put them in sequence on the washing line.
    - Make their own books and sequence.

TOP TIP
Visit charity shops or libraries to get duplicate copies of children's books.

Puppet fun

This core activity is suitable for a one or a small group of children.

What you need:

A quiet uninterrupted space

Large floor cushions

A selection of socks or gloves or brown paper bags

Round stickers and a marker pen

A selection of buttons, felt, glue, needle and thread

Enhancing the activity

- Use children's gloves/mittens to make individual puppets for children to use during the session.

♪ Sing songs about what your story is about. If you can't remember one, make up a song or have a songbook at hand to look at. You could sing Tommy Thumb.

Puppets are a great way of communicating with children and will enhance any story time session. Puppets are so much fun and will engage children during any story especially when dealing with feelings. You don't have to buy expensive puppets, why not make your own? In this version, the adult makes the simple puppets, as the focus is on using them for communication!

What you do

These puppets are not a craft activity! They are for language and communication work, so make them before you use them with the children. Decorate the socks yourself by drawing eyes on the round stickers and sticking them on the socks. If time allows, you can be more creative by sewing on buttons and material to make the eyes, a mouth, the tongue and hair.

1 Sit on the cushions with the children and gently introduce the puppet or puppets.
2 Observe the children's responses to the puppets.
3 Use the puppet to talk to the children and 'make up a story'. This can be about what has happened that day or to accompany a storybook.
4 Encourage the children to join in the story and make decisions about the direction the puppet takes.
5 Praise the children for joining in and offer support and extra reassurance for children who are not so confident.

Key words and gestures

- Use of the children's name
- Use gesture and facial expression to reinforce what you say: 'Shall we have some fun?' 'Are you ready?' 'What have I got here?' 'What do you think they are?' 'Let's put the puppet on to your hand?' 'Is it soft?' 'Is that you?' 'Shall we make a puppet?' 'Let's do it again' 'Did you enjoy that?' 'Listen' 'Let's...'
- Use different voice tones to keep the children's attention.

Involving parents

You could...
- Show parents how easily puppets can be made at home using socks or tights.

Look, listen and note

Does the child…
- *Use a range of language such as describing words, object words, action words and prepositions?*
- *Interact with other children, copying, taking turns and sharing?*
- *Use his/her imagination through storytelling?*
- *Stay engaged? For how long?*
- *Genuinely interact with the puppets as you or they use them?*

Extending the challenge

- Have a prop box or bag full of different types of puppet.
- Make puppets for your favourite stories – a green sock can easily be made in to *The Very Hungry Caterpillar*.
- For older children:
    - Encourage the children to make up stories using the puppets.
    - Do a puppet show together.

Take it outside

- Puppets are easily transferred to outside play either independently or as a small group.
- Place a blanket under a tree with some cushions to make the perfect area to have fun with puppets.
- Always put static activities such as this in a shady place to avoid accidental over-exposure to the sun.

TOP TIP
Use puppets softly and gently, some children may be frightened of them at first.

Books and songs

Children love books and should have the opportunity to experience books on a daily basis, both on their own and with a familiar adult. Have a basket containing a range of suitable books for the children to look through. Encourage them to choose which story they would like to have.

Before you read the book ensure that you and the child/children are sitting comfortably in a warm, quiet environment and that you are familiar with the book before you start.

A selection of suitable books:

The Tiger Who Came For Tea by Judith Kerr
(Harper Collins)

Dogger by Shirley Hughes
(Red Fox Books)

Whatever Next by Jill Murphey
(Macmillian Books)

Elmer by David McKee
(Anderson Press)

Kipper by Mick Inkpen
(Hodder Children's Books)

The Very Busy Spider by Eric Carle
(Puffin Books)

Rainbow Fish by Marcus Pfister
(North South Books)

Each, Peach, Pear Thumb by Allan Ahlberg and Janet Ahlberg
(Puffin Books)

Peace At Last by Jill Murphy
(Campbell Books)

Brown Bear, Brown Bear What Do You See?
by Bill Martin Jr and Eric Carle
(Puffin Books)

Lost and Found by Oliver Jeffers
(Harper Collins)

The Gingerbread Man
(Ladybird Favourite Tales)

Hairy Maclary and Zachery Quack by Lynley Dodd
(Puffin Books)

Ten Chuckling Ducklings by Sally Crabtree and Sally Hobson
(Scholastic)

Happy Birthday Moon by Frank Asch
(Picture Corgi Books)

Penguin Small by Mick Inkpen
(Hodder Children's Books)

The Enormous Turnip
(Ladybird Favourite Tales)

Farmer Duck by Martin Waddle
(Walker Books)

Songs and rhymes are a well-tried way of communicating with children and you can sing songs at any time of the day.

A selection of suitable songs:

Wind the Bobbin
Wind the bobbin up, wind the bobbin up
Pull, pull, clap, clap, clap
Point to the ceiling, point to the floor,
Point to the window, point to the door
Clap your hands together, one, two, three
And lay them gently on your knee
(Act out the actions to match the song)

If You're Happy and You Know It
If you're happy and you know it, clap your hands,
If you're happy and you know it, clap your hands,
If you're happy and you know it and you really want to tell us,
If you're happy and you know it, clap your hands
If you're happy and you know it: stamp your feet
nod your head shout 'we are'
(Act out the actions to match the song)

Old MacDonald had a farm
Old MacDonald had a farm, E-I-E-I-O
And on that farm, he had a pig, E-I-E-I-O
With a oink, oink here, and a oink, oink there,
Here a oink, there a oink, everywhere a oink oink.
Old MacDonald had a farm, E-I-E-I-O
(Use different animals and the sounds they make)

Down in the jungle
Down in the jungle where the tall grass grows,
There's a great big gorilla washing his clothes,
With a rub-a-dub here, rub-a-dub there,
That's the way he washes his clothes.
Boobady boom-boom, boogie-woogie, woogie
Boobady boom-boom, boogie-woogie, woogie
Boobady boom-boom, boogie-woogie, woogie
That's the way he washes his clothes

Up the tall white candlestick
Up the tall white candlestick, went little mousie brown,
Right to the top, but he couldn't get down,
So he called for his Grandma

Grandma, Grandma
But Grandma was in town
So he curled himself in to a ball and rolled himself down
(Act out the actions to match the song)

The Wheels on the Bus
The wheels on the bus go round and round,
round and round, round and round
The wheels on the bus go round and round all day long.

The horn on the bus goes beep, beep, beep
The wipers on the bus go swish, swish, swish
The conductor on the bus says move along please
The mummies on the bus go chatter, chatter, chatter

5 Little Ducks
5 little ducks went swimming one day, over the pond and far away,
Mummy duck said 'quack, quack, quack'
But only 4 little ducks came swimming back.

4 little ducks
3 little ducks
2 little ducks

1 little ducks went swimming one day, over the pond and far away,
Mummy duck said 'quack, quack, quack'
And 5 little ducks came swimming back.
(Use your fingers to count down the ducks)

The farmer's in his den
The farmer's in his den, the farmer's in his den,
E-I-E-I, the farmer's in his den.

The farmer wants a wife
The wife wants a child
The child wants a nurse
The nurse wants a dog
We all pat the dog
(Stand in a circle, choose a farmer and walk around the farmer singing the song. The farmer chooses a wife, the wife chooses a child etc)

let's **talk** about

Weather

ISBN 978-1-4081-2668-4

let's **talk** about
Toys

ISBN 978-1-4081-2667-7

let's **talk** about
the Park

ISBN 978-1-4081-2669-1

let's **talk** about
Farms

ISBN 978-1-4081-2666-0

This exciting new series covers the six EYFS areas of learning and development through a variety of age appropriate themes. It fulfils the aims of the Every Child a Talker initiative.

Let's talk about... provides practitioners and children with entertaining, exciting and stimulating language activities that foster and enhance early language learning.